Berlitz®

South Africa

D1370657

Berlitz

South Africa

Text by Martin Gostelow and Ken Bernstein
Updated by Melissa de Villiers
Edited by Romily Hambling
Photography: Erling Mandelmann, Chris Coe,
South African Tourism
Cover photograph South African Tourism
Layout: Media Content Marketing, Inc.
Series Editor: Tony Halliday

Third Edition 1998 (updated 2003)

CONTACTING THE EDITORS
Every effort has been made to provide accurate information in this publication, but changes are inevitable. The publisher cannot be responsible for any resulting loss, inconvenience or injury. We would appreciate it if readers would call our attention to any errors or outdated information by contacting Berlitz Publishing, PO Box 7910, London SE1 1WE, England. Fax: (44) 20 7403 0290;
e-mail: berlitz@apaguide.co.uk; www.berlitzpublishing.com

070/303 REV

CONTENTS

• A ☛ in the text denotes a highly recommended sight

South Africa

SOUTH AFRICA AND THE SOUTH AFRICANS

You have to see it to believe it. Just as beautiful as everyone says, and with the seasons conveniently reversed to make it a perfect escape from Northern Hemisphere winters, South Africa is now more accessible than ever before.

South Africans are keen travellers in their own country and expect high standards, so facilities are generally excellent. After a day in the game parks, playing golf or seeing the sights, you can expect a generous dinner and a bottle of good local wine. Air-conditioning, colour televisions and all modern conveniences are close at hand. And no matter where you go, you can drink the water from the tap.

South Africa is the undisputed powerhouse and economic giant of the African continent, with massive industrial and mining enterprises, but the Africa of legends and dreams is all around you. In Kruger National Park alone, 122 species of mammal and 495 of bird are protected but not pampered. Along many ordinary roads, the sight of antelope, ostriches and freely roaming monkeys is commonplace. There are as many 'Do not feed the baboons' signs here as 'Keep off the grass'.

Bigger than California and Texas combined, South Africa calls to mind the same feeling of wide-open spaces. Some of the sights are similar: spectacular coastlines, vineyards and orchards, moody deserts, cities with glossy skyscrapers, suburbs full of long, low, white houses, and sleepy country towns. Away from the cities, petrol stations can be so far apart you are loath to pass one by. When you stop, people will eye you with friendly curiosity. When you get into conversation, you'll usually be asked: 'What do you think of South Africa?'

One of South Africa's elegant Cape Dutch mansions.

South Africa

Once you've set aside preconceptions, it is likely that your judgments will be as varied as the scenery and the population. Consider half a dozen archetypal citizens: one is a post office clerk with a harsh Afrikaans accent, stoking the charcoal for the beloved *braai* (barbecue); another is a very British lady, distinctive in her white hat and playing bowls on a fanatically trimmed lawn. The Zulu farmer who tills the parched soil lives in a different world from his cousin digging for gold under Johannesburg. The Cape Coloured bank teller thinks in Afrikaans; the Indian entrepreneur in Durban speaks a clipped English; and yet all are natives of the same South Africa, members of a mosaic of peoples making up a whole world of differences in one land. How they all get along together is a matter of great concern, which has made this one

> **Besides Africaans and English there are nine official languages in South Africa.**

Spectacular coastlines and beautiful beaches are among the many varied landscapes of South Africa.

of the most controversial countries in the world.

The rich diversity of the population extends to almost every other aspect of life in South Africa. Landscapes range from rainforest to semi-desert, to plantations of pine and eucalyptus and rows of stately palms. Flowers of the most romantic extremes flourish at one altitude or another. The architecture, also, is quite as varied and includes 'beehive' huts, looking like tropical igloos, graceful Cape Dutch mansions all in white and the sky-

In Kruger National Park, zebras cavort amid typical bushveld scenery.

scrapers of finance corporations and wealthy multinationals.

Thanks to a veritable explosion in the international tourist market over the last 10 years, a large number of international carriers now fly direct to the country. A non-stop flight from London to Johannesburg – around 9,700km (6,000 miles) – takes about 11 hours.

From the late 1940s, when the policy of apartheid (separateness) was codified, successive South African governments pursued the goal of separate development of racial groups. This entailed the mass removal of citizens to new housing areas, a ban on marriage between whites and non-whites and the segregation of schools, hotels, buses, trains and even park benches. These laws have now been repealed, the government finally admitting that apartheid had been continued long after it had been proved unworkable.

Fewer than one in five of South Africa's 40 million inhabitants are white. The majority – two out of three – are black, belonging to a number of nations or tribes, the biggest of which are the Zulu, Xhosa, Sotho and Tswana. Just over 10 percent of the population is referred to as Coloured, meaning of mixed race. Another 3.3 percent are Asian, mostly the descendants of immigrants from India. Incidentally, white South Africans object strongly to being considered mere settlers or immigrants in Africa, especially those whose roots go back more than three centuries to the foundation of the Dutch station at the Cape. With them the Dutch language was introduced and from it evolved Afrikaans, the mother tongue of most South African whites and Coloured people. Nearly 40 percent of whites are native English-speakers and English is understood almost everywhere.

South Africa looks out to two oceans (the Atlantic and the Indian) and five countries: Namibia (formerly known as South West Africa), Botswana, Zimbabwe, Mozambique and Swaziland. In addition, the 30,355-sq km (11,720-sq mile) independent Kingdom of Lesotho is surrounded by South African territory.

Since the elections of April 1994 and subsequent changes, South Africa has become a unitary, integrated state, incorporating the former so-called 'independent republics' and 'homelands,' including Transkei and Venda. The country is divided into nine administrative provinces, each with its own limited powers, governed by a parliament consisting of a lower house and a senate.

Though the map is a jigsaw, the country is held together by first-class communications. The roads are good and include some handsome motorways. Domestic air services link all the sizeable towns, while the rail network ranges from quaint local services to the super-luxurious Blue Train.

You can see South Africa by any combination of car, train and plane, or hire a caravan (trailer) and take your hotel along with you; caravan parks are well equipped and often set in admirable locations. Alternatively, abandon the driving and the decisions and join an organised coach tour. It's all a question of available time and your taste, but you'll want to strike a balance between the cities and the countryside and between culture and nature.

Arrive by air at Johannesburg and you'll soon notice that it is a wheeler-dealer city of skyscrapers, built on gold both literally and metaphorically: those sandy little mountains surrounding the city are waste heaps from the original gold mines. Less than 65km (40 miles) north is the administrative capital, Pretoria, an especially attractive place in September or October, when its thousands of jacaranda trees flower.

Over on the Indian Ocean, the city of Durban, Africa's largest port, is also a lively beach resort and surfing centre.

A field of sunflowers in KwaZulu-Natal is just one aspect of South Africa's natural beauty .

Most of its inhabitants are of Indian origin, helping to give the city some spicy cosmopolitan overtones.

Beautifully set between the Atlantic and the unforgettable landmark of Table Mountain, Cape Town (founded in 1652) is known affectionately as the 'mother city'. Few would disagree that this is the fairest South African city of them all, and within easy reach is one of Africa's best-known natural attractions, the Cape of Good Hope, where the 'end-of-the-world' seascape makes for high drama.

When it comes to natural wonders, nothing beats South Africa's game sanctuaries and the thrill of discovering and photographing lions, rhinos, hippos and buffaloes going about their daily lives. They're often so near that you won't need a telephoto lens or binoculars except for spying the shyer creatures. What's more, while waiting for the bigger game, you will also develop a new awareness of the flowers, trees, birds and butterflies. Everybody succumbs to the magic of South Africa's natural kingdom.

The sports possibilities cover a lot of ground (golf, hiking, horse riding) as well as a lot of ocean (fishing, surfing, swimming). Rugby, cricket, football, boxing and horse racing draw the big crowds. As for nightlife and entertainment, South Africa's cities offer theatres, concerts, ballet, cinemas, nightclubs and discotheques. The restaurants are notable not only for gargantuan portions but for quality meats and seafoods, salads and fresh fruits. Cape wines can be superb and even the more modest varieties are invariably drinkable and well priced.

The shopping choices range from the American-style air-conditioned malls to colourful street markets. As souvenirs you might want to take home some wood carvings, weavings, or painting – the work of local artists and artisans.

The bustle of commerce in Durban's Indian market.

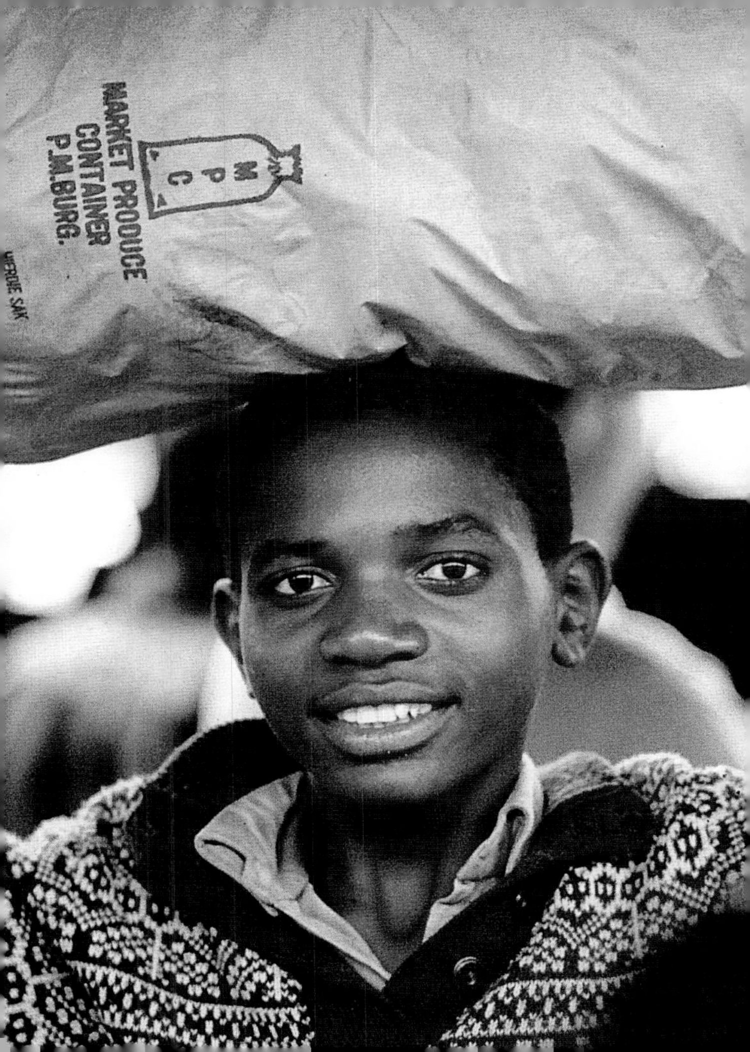
MARKET PRODUCE
CONTAINER
P.M.BURG.
M P C

A BRIEF HISTORY

South Africa came late to the pages of recorded history, but it seems that our own species, Homo sapiens, first evolved on its sunny upland plains. Long before that, about 1,800,000 years ago, a type of ape-man known as *Australopithecus africanus* lived scarcely 30km (20 miles) northwest of the site where Johannesburg is now situated. Other fossil bones show that by 50,000 years ago a family that was recognisably human inhabited caves in Mpumalonga Province. Able to use fire and stone tools, these people were probably the ancestors of the hunter-gatherers responsible for the vivid rock paintings found all over southern Africa.

By the fifth century AD, migrating tribes from West Africa had brought an Iron-Age culture to the country's northern reaches. When Europeans first came to the southern tip of Africa they met other early inhabitants of the area – smaller, lighter-skinned people who hunted or herded cattle. They called the cattle-herders Hottentots, while the hunters were known as Bushmen. Today they are classified as Khoikhoi and San, or given the composite name Khoisan.

When the first European settlers arrived in the mid-17th century, several black nations had migrated from the centre of the continent to southern Africa. There was little contact between them and the white settlers at the Cape until the mid-18th century. The Khoikhoi began to act as middle-men, but their numbers soon declined through war and disease until they finally faded away, blending into what has since become known as the Cape Coloured population.

The Dutch at the Cape

Portuguese explorers had been rounding the Cape of Good Hope (they first called it the Cape of Storms) since the end

San Rock art depicts the early inhabitants of South Africa.

of the 15th century. For European ships, especially Dutch, the Cape became a regular port of call where they could take on fresh water and barter iron, beads and brandy in exchange for local cattle. Sixty Dutch crew were forced to spend almost a year at the Cape when their ship was driven ashore in 1647. Once home, their leaders recommended setting up a permanent settlement to provide facilities for ships of the Dutch East Indies Company on the way to and from their possessions in Southeast Asia.

On 7 April 1652, a party of about 100 under the command of Jan van Riebeeck landed at Table Bay and set about building a fort and preparing land for growing food. There were inevitable clashes with the Khoikhoi, whose grazing lands were infringed upon, but the intended task of provisioning visiting ships was achieved.

The colony kept its Dutch character even after the arrival of other nationalities, most of whom were French Huguenot refugees (who added expertise to the Cape wine industry). The immigrants were obliged to learn the Dutch language but they brought a special fervour to the Calvinist tone of the colony's official Dutch Reformed Church. A new people, the Afrikaners, or Boers (from the Dutch word *boer*, for farmer), was being forged. Pushing farther into the interior, many of them paid little heed to the authorities in Cape Castle, still less to those back in Amsterdam.

Enter the British

Wars in Europe sent shock waves as far as South Africa. After a French attack on the Netherlands, the British occupied the Cape colony in 1795. They returned first in 1806 and again, definitively, in 1814 as a result of exchanges of territory following the Napoleonic wars. The change of management shook the foundations of Cape society. Britain outlawed the slave trade in 1807, going on to abolish slavery throughout the Empire in 1836. Faced with a curtailed labour supply, with little or no compensation and the imposition of the English language and legal system, many colonials began to strike out on their own into the wilderness. The pioneers became known as the Voortrekkers (literally, 'those who move the front').

Ritual Zulu dances.

Much of the land they took had been abandoned not long before as a result of Zulu raids on other tribes, and the Boers forced their wagon trains deep into the heart of the subcontinent. A new British colony on the Indian Ocean coast of Natal restricted the Voortrekkers to the interior, where they established two new states: the Orange Free State between the rivers Orange and Vaal and the Transvaal Republic to the north of the Vaal.

Citing chaotically bad government and ill treatment of the black population, in 1877 the British took the Transvaal. Encouraged by the news of a British defeat at the hands of the Zulus in Natal, however, the Transvaalers rose against their occupiers and forced the British to withdraw in 1881. The clash of British and Boer interests grated quietly until the turn of the century, when it exploded in a second, much longer and more bitter war.

Fighting between white settlers and black tribes had continued on and off since the second half of the 18th century. Frontier wars with the Xhosa, for example, were fought every 10 years or so. The struggle for usable land also underlay wars of black against black, the most dramatic being those waged by Zulu general Shaka, known as 'the black Napoleon', who died in 1828. As time went on, Zulu leaders fought the Voortrekkers, then the British and it was only in the 1880s that British firepower imposed a kind of peace.

Glittering Hopes

In Hopetown, on the Orange River, the first diamond was discovered in 1866. The area was invaded by fortune hunters after a giant stone of 83.5 carats appeared, and the action soon shifted north to Kimberley, where finding diamonds was almost easy. Over the next 40 years, diggers went ever deeper, until Kimberley's Big Hole had yielded 3 tons of diamonds.

Gold had been found in various parts of South Africa, but the big strike came in the Transvaal in 1886 on the highveld referred to as the Witwatersrand, or Rand for short, which subsequently became the site of Johannesburg. The prospector sold his claim for £10 and was never heard of again; the reef he found has since come up with more than 35,000 metric tons (32,000 tons) of pure gold.

Since 1881 Britain had kept her distance from events in the independent Transvaal, claiming only a vague right of veto over external alliances. However, with the Rand's riches unearthed, foreign prospectors and entrepreneurs flocked in, very quickly outnumbering the descendants of the Voortrekkers.

The republic's government benefited from the taxes and duties levied on the *uitlanders* (foreigners) but denied them any voice in running the country. Cecil Rhodes, the mining magnate and prime minister of Cape Colony, plotted an uprising of the Transvaal *uitlanders*, but his accomplice, Dr Jameson, jumped the gun by leading an invading party from Rhodesia. His ragtag column was quickly overcome by the more substantially armed Boers, and the leaders were subsequently put on trial. Three years later, in 1899, the British and the Afrikaners fought the issue out in the open.

The Anglo–Boer War

The Afrikaners were led at this time by the long-established president of the Transvaal – the bearded, top-hatted Paul Kruger. Three of his prominent military chiefs, Louis Botha, Jan Smuts and J.B.M. Hertzog, were destined to become prime ministers of the Union of South Africa. Although initially outnumbered by a ratio of five to one, the Boers held their own through innovative commando tactics.

The methods of British strategist Lord Kitchener were harsh. Families of Boer soldiers were incarcerated in concentration camps. A total of 26,000 inmates died, mostly of disease. Much less publicised were the conditions in separate camps the British built for blacks, where the death toll was over 13,000. The revelations shocked British opinion and strengthened the inward-looking Afrikaners.

After two and a half years of fighting, the Boers conceded defeat in May 1902. Shortly after this, Britain agreed to the formation of a self-governing dominion, but despite this gesture, they managed to alienate the Afrikaners and did not attempt to extend to the Transvaal even the limited rights of non-whites that existed in the Cape and Natal.

The Union of South Africa, created in 1910, was an amalgam of the Transvaal and Orange Free State with the Cape and Natal, Britain's two colonies. So delicate were regional sensibilities that power bases were spread around the country, with Pretoria the administrative capital, Bloemfontein the judicial capital and Cape Town the seat of Parliament. Foreshadowing future policies it was decided that only whites could be elected as members of parliament.

The World Wars and Aftermath

Only four years after creating the Union of South Africa the British Empire went to war with Germany. South African troops were quick to seize the German colony of South West Africa and took a major part in the long campaign against German-led forces in East Africa.

By the time World War II broke out, Jan Smuts was in his second term as prime minister. Beating a powerful parliamentary minority in favour of neutrality, he led his country into the war against Nazi Germany. South African troops thus entered the fray in North Africa and Italy.

Although Smuts drafted the human rights declaration of the United Nations charter, South Africa was almost immediately under fire for its own human rights record and the country ended up pulling out of the UN agencies. Under pressure from the multi-racial Commonwealth, South Africa withdrew from its historical relationship with Britain, becoming an independent republic in 1961. Western nations imposed trade embargos, especially on military equipment.

Society under Tension

The policies by which South Africa became regarded as an international pariah were encapsulated by the Afrikaans word *apartheid* (translated as 'separateness'). The term took on international currency after the election of the National Party government in 1948, as the web of laws for racial separation and control was woven ever tighter.

Violent protests against apartheid, along with the government's reaction to the unrest, kept South Africa in the international spotlight. In 1960 opposition to the pass laws, which affected all blacks, culminated in a demonstration at Sharpeville, in the Transvaal, when the police opened fire on the crowd, killing 69 blacks and wounding 178. In 1976, in Soweto, violence brought 176 deaths and more than a thousand injured. Following this, the government placed a ban on individuals and organisations suspected of subversion.

New unrest sweeping the townships during the mid-1980s prompted a state of emergency. Thousands, almost all blacks, were arrested and then held without trial. Violence dominated television screens abroad until news crews were finally barred.

Under growing internal and external pressures the government changed direction dramatically and decided to scrap much of the legal structure of apartheid. In 1990 President

F.W. de Klerk legalised the African National Congress and other previously banned organisations and ANC leader Nelson Mandela was released after 27 historic years in prison.

The memorable elections in April 1994 were relayed round the world as a 'miracle of democracy'. Nelson Mandela came to power as president at the head of the ANC, in a government of national unity.

Voted back into (sole) power with a comfortable majority in the 1999 elections, the ANC still has a great deal of prestige, although it is clear that Mandela's successor, Thabo Mbeki, faces some tough challenges. While major social and economic reform is underway – and has

Nelson Mandela made history as South Africa's first black president.

become the government's top priority – foreign investment has been slow to materialise. What's more, violent crime has increased, further discouraging investment. Nonetheless, at last South Africa has a democratic constitution, which allows blacks to study, work and move freely in their own country. The world continues to watch with hope as a crucial new era unfolds.

WHERE TO GO

The size of France, Germany, Holland, and Belgium combined, South Africa is clearly too big to get to know in a single visit. In the following pages we set out the highlights to help you choose an itinerary.

We begin in Johannesburg, the largest and most dynamic city in the republic, sprawling across a plateau nearby 2km (1 mile) above sea level. After a look at nearby Pretoria, with a diversion to Sun City, we head for Mpumalanga Province and South Africa's prime tourist attraction, the Kruger National Park. Crossing the mountains of KwaZulu-Natal, we come to bustling Durban on the Indian Ocean and take a trip north into Zululand. Then

A member of Johannesburg's younger generation enjoys a comfortable ride.

we jump to Port Elizabeth and follow the coast clockwise along the Garden Route and all the way to Cape Town, which becomes our base for visits to the Cape of Good Hope itself and to the Cape wine country. Finally, we complete the circle by looking at various ways back to Johannesburg: the luxurious Blue Train; the long drive across the Great Karoo to Kimberley; or still farther north to the fringes of the Kalahari Desert.

Inevitably, we have had to

Views over Johannesburg.

leave out large areas that require more leisurely exploration. These, of course, merit a return trip to South Africa.

JOHANNESBURG

Most of the world's great cities were built next to rivers, but Johannesburg has an underground stream – of gold. That was enough to transform it in three years from meagre grazing land to the biggest town in South Africa. A century later it is a metropolis which, with its suburbs and satellites, is home to more than three million people.

You can tell that gold made this city. Streets have names like Claim and Nugget and it is impossible to miss the artificial hills, which look like transplants from outer space. In recent years, most of the dumps have been cleared and reprocessed to extract the gold left behind by old techniques.

The 1890s look has been re-created in Gold Reef City, which is southwest of Johannesburg (see pages 30–1).

Some of the pioneering pace survives, with pedestrians still bustling about as if hurrying to stake a claim. Some attribute this animation to the altitude – almost 1,750 metres (5,740 ft). But some visitors tire easily.

Johannesburg is at its best in summer (from November to March). Warm, sunny mornings may turn into thundery afternoons, but the torrential rains soon move on, leaving the city refreshed and the countryside green. In the winter, however, the dry winds are cold and the grass turns brown.

Like every one of South Africa's cities, Johannesburg's population patterns were dislocated by the racial separation laws (since repealed, but their effect remains). Thus, some 50,000 Asians were resettled in their own suburb, Lenasia, and the blacks assigned to vast townships on the outskirts. Soweto, by far the biggest, is home to what estimates put at more than two million people, many of whom commute each morning to work in the city.

City Centre

Downtown Johannesburg is a colourful mix of skyscrapers casting tall shadows over Indian bazaars and traditional African *muti* (medicine) shops, where smart-suited office workers rub shoulders with beggars and hawkers. It is also one of the city's worst areas for street crime, so don't go out on the streets here carrying a camera or wearing an expensive watch or pair of sunglasses. Also, don't carry more money than you actually need.

Smal Street is a pedestrian shopping area. Throughout the city centre a relaxation of restrictions on street trading has resulted in hundreds of hawkers setting up market stalls or simply spreading a cloth on the ground and selling every imaginable commodity. Africa has come to South Africa's financial hub.

Among all the office buildings it's hard to find many historical monuments (which, in this city, means anything older than World War I), but local preservationists are proud of the **Rissik Street Post Office**, begun in 1897. After the Anglo–Boer War, the red-brick building was given an extra floor and a clock tower.

The **Johannesburg Public Library**, in a small park behind the colonnaded City Hall, is the country's biggest. The first floor houses a fine collection of geological specimens, including gold- and diamond-bearing ores.

Over in Bree Street is the **Newtown Cultural Precinct**, a former fruit and vegetable market. Here you will find the **MuseuMAfrica**, with a range of exhibits on black African history and culture, including a small section on the San and Khoikhoi people *(see page 14)*. Displays include full-sized tribal huts, utensils, jewellery, musical instruments, weapons and costumes. Stone Age paintings depict animals and hunters with great sophistication. Visit a Bushman cave complete with all the authentic sounds of daily life, or, for a more contemporary experience, a township shack constructed of tin and cardboard. A section of the museum highlights the history of the white settlers, with a good collection of Cape silver and sturdy pioneer furniture. A Victorian pub and pharmacy have been reconstructed. The museum is closed on Monday.

Also in the Cultural Precinct is a beer museum, opened in 1995; tastings are included in the entrance fee.

The other end of the long building houses the **Market Theatre** complex, which includes exhibition space and a

In cafés you can buy non-alcoholic drinks and food to take away. There is no seating.

children's play area. Outside, the car park is transformed on Saturdays into a cheerful and popular flea market.

To the west of the Newtown market a big concrete shopping centre in vaguely Moghul style called **Oriental Plaza** stretches from Bree Street to Main Street. The smell of spices greets you before you arrive. Connecting courtyards are ringed by Indian restaurants, snack bars and shops.

The city's **railway station**, Africa's largest, was built in the 1960s in true grand style. Before the repeal of apartheid laws, non-whites used a separate part of the building and travelled in separate carriages. Every day some 200,000 black people arrive here by train from Soweto. In marked contrast, the luxury Blue Train *(see page 83)* leaves for Cape Town from here.

The 'Hillbrow Tower' is one of Johannesburg's best known landmarks.

The old concourse houses the **South African Transport Museum**, which displays such memorabilia as a real 1890 locomotive and model trains, planes and ships. Gadgets and details include platform-ticket machines, lanterns, dining-car place settings and switching control panels.

Housed in a building designed by Sir Edwin

Lutyens, the **Johannesburg Art Gallery** (closed on Monday) is set in Joubert Park, the city's oldest park, east of the railway station. The collection starts off with El Greco and 17th-century Dutch painters, but most space is devoted to the 19th and early 20th centuries. There's a rich vein of the work of the Pre-Raphaelites and their followers, including Sir John Millais, G.F. Watts and Dante Gabriel Rossetti. Among a good variety of Impressionists and Post-Impressionists, works by Sisley, Signac, Bonnard and Pissarro stand out. A small

South Africa's colourful street markets offer fresh produce and plenty more.

but representative display of South African art brings the show up to date – look for landscapes by Jan Pierneef (1886–1957). Guided tours of the gallery are available.

An unusual **monument** stands at the top of Rissik Street, a few blocks north of the railway station statues of three gold miners – two black and one white – at work with a big pneumatic drill.

Beyond it, the **Civic Centre** (with a novel triangular floor plan) is a hive of municipal activity. Alongside, the modern **Civic Theatre** stages drama, opera and ballet.

Westwards lie the campuses of Johannesburg's two universities. The **University of the Witwatersrand** (Wits for

The unusual three-miners statue was donated to the city by the Chamber of Mines.

short – pronounced Vits) is Africa's biggest English-language university. In front of the university library is the original **cross** which the famous Portuguese explorer Bartolomeu Dias put up near Port Elizabeth in 1488. To the west of Wits is the modern campus of **Rand Afrikaans University**.

North of the Centre

Called the tallest structure in Africa, the **J. G. Strijdom Tower** is a communications relay post 269 metres (882ft) high. The functional design included an observation desk, but the tower is no longer open to the public, closed for security reasons. The tower rises above **Hillbrow**, the most racially mixed Johannesburg neighbourhood and one with an animated nightlife – although you're advised not to walk alone either here or in the Central Business District after dark. More ornamental than the Strijdom Tower, Johannesburg's other tower, in Brixton, belongs to the South African Broadcasting Corporation.

The **National Museum of Military History** (which was formerly the War Museum) stands in Hermann Ekstein Park in the northern suburb of Saxonwold. Plenty of military hardware is on show, from old-time flintlocks to World War II tanks, as well as battle flags, uniforms and medals. A collection of historic aircraft includes a Spitfire, a Hurricane and a Mosquito, along with a real rarity: the two-seat night-fighter version of the Messerschmidt 262, the world's first combat jet. Johannesburg's modest but pleasant **zoo** is in the same park area, the zoo lake is occasionally the site of informal art displays on Sundays.

Far enough north of the Central Business District to be a separate municipality, fashionable **Sandton City** has some of the best hotels in the area and a shopping complex claimed to be the biggest and finest in the southern hemisphere.

Southwestern Outskirts

You might want to take a tour of **Soweto**, which makes a striking contrast to the prosperous northern suburbs. The Soweto City Council runs bus tours on Monday to Friday mornings, starting from the Carlton Centre. They must be booked in advance; contact the Gduteng Tourist Authority, tel: 327-2000. Private tour companies also operate trips to Soweto.

'Soweto' sounds African, but it's really just a contraction of South Western Townships, where some 2 million black people live in small, cramped houses. The tours pass through the neighbourhoods, though there are stops at a model kindergarten, a folklore park and a modern shopping centre run by blacks. Contrasting with most of the townships are the new sub-divisions of middle-class black housing and the exclusive streets known as Millionaires' Row. Due to the high crime rate, you should stick to the organised tours and forego any adventures there on your own.

The site of 14 Shaft of Crown Mines in Alamein Road, southwest of the city centre, is now the focus of **Gold Reef City**, a theme park with fairground rides, shows, bars and a fine hotel, all in the style of the 1890s, as well as restaurants and many shops. The highlight for most visitors is a 40-

Soweto stands in sharp contrast to Johannesburg and its prosperous northern suburbs.

minute trip through a real **gold mine** – going down a shaft to a level 220 metres (722ft) below ground, decked out in protective gear and miners' lamps. There's even an underground pub, housed in a former donkey stable. Children aged 6 and over are allowed to go along, although some of the younger ones may be unsettled by the claustrophobia and darkness of half an hour below the surface and by the loud noise of demonstration drilling.

The mine was once one of the world's richest, employing no fewer than 30,000 people. Then, when the economic ore deposits had been worked out, the South African Chamber of Mines established the **mining museum** that is now the centrepiece of Gold Reef City. The story of gold is well illustrated and visitors are shown around a replica of an early miners' village and a working model of a gold-processing system. You will see real molten gold being poured into a mould of a 25-kg (55-lb) ingot. Once it has cooled visitors are allowed to pose with their hands on the bar, which is worth about a quarter of a million dollars.

South Africa's gold mines employ about 250,000 underground workers, mostly black contract labourers recruited in neighbouring countries. Every Sunday, miners from one of the regions don skins and feathers and perform **tribal dances** in an amphitheatre at Gold Reef City. Dances include the famous Isicathulu, or 'Gumboot' dance.

Visits to working mines can be organised through the Chamber of Mines, tel: 498-7100.

Right next to the Gold Reef City complex is the new **Museum of Apartheid** (closed on Monday; not suitable for children under 12). As the name implies, it sets out to illustrate apartheid's grim story and demonstrate the perilous results of racial prejudice; this is achieved through graphic photographs, film footage and imaginative installations, including a police 'Casspir' once used to patrol the townships. To book a tour, tel: 496-1822.

Gold Reef's mining museum illustrates the story of gold mining and processing.

Midrand, halfway between Johannesburg and Pretoria, is a huge complex combining shopping malls, cinemas and other entertainment opportunities. It's worth a look if you have an afternoon to spare.

PRETORIA

In the spring (October and November) the garden city of Pretoria shimmers in a purple haze as 60,000 jacaranda trees imported from Brazil bloom in a spectacle of delicate beauty. You'll find Pretoria an agreeable place at any time, though, with beautiful parks and some innovative architecture.

The metropolitan area has a population of about 750,000. Unlike other major cities in South Africa, Pretoria has a majority of whites, many of them working in government jobs, for this is currently the administrative capital of the republic, though its future status hangs in the balance.

Pretoria's historic heart is **Church Square**, where early settlers built their first church in the 1850s. A statue of Paul Kruger – the craggy patriarch who was elected president four times in the late 19th century – stands in the middle of the square. Around the base of the monument are statues of four citizen-soldiers of the era. Photographers equipped with instant cameras stake out this spot, waiting to snap tourists with the statues as a backdrop, then sell them the photos.

Some distinguished official buildings from earlier days face the square: the old **Raadsaal** (parliament), in Italian Renaissance style; the old **South African Reserve Bank**, designed by Sir Herbert Baker; and the **Palace of Justice**, used as a hospital during the British occupation of 1900. Among the adventurous modern buildings near the square that have lifted the skyline is the **Volkskas-sentrum**, headquarters of the first Afrikaner-controlled bank.

Strijdom Square, located just down the street from the Volkskas skyscraper, honours J.G. Strijdom, prime minister in the 1950s, with a bust that is about 12 times life size. Adjoining the square is the **State Theatre complex,** which comprises six auditoria and may be viewed on guided tours *(see page 119).* A couple of blocks away up Van der Walt Street, a huge municipal office building, the Munitoria, contains the Information Bureau, which hands out local maps, leaflets and advice.

If you really can't manage a trip to a game park, you might look in at Pretoria's **National Zoological Gardens,** around 3,500 species displayed in showy flower gardens; a cable car floats above some areas. Next door, the **National Cultural History and Open Air Museum** (closed Saturday morning and Sunday) has something for everyone, from Stone Age

Bright modern buildings raise the skyline of the beautiful garden capital of Pretoria.

rock engravings to a replica of General Smuts's bedroom. On show are old wagons and cannon and a room full of historic bibles. The hoard of 18th-century silver bowls, pots and pitchers from the Cape Colony is one of the best in the nation.

Sir Herbert Baker designed Pretoria's noblest architectural ensemble, the **Union Buildings**, a couple of mirror-image structures linked by a semi-circular colonnade. This big ministerial complex, the site of President Mandela's inauguration in 1994, looks down on formal gardens (open to the public) of brilliant flowers, sculpted trees and flawless lawns.

Bird-watchers don't know which way to turn in South Africa, where even suburban gardens harbour the most exotic birds in wild colour schemes. For a rapid initiation try the **Transvaal Museum** in Paul Kruger Street, where every

Pretoria's Union Buildings were designed by celebrated British colonial architect, Sir Herbert Baker.

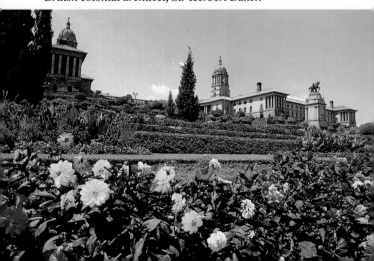

species of South African bird is identified. Among other educational devices, there is a sort of jukebox for birdcalls. As a national research organisation the museum also covers butterflies, reptiles and other aspects of natural history.

Southern Outskirts

South of Pretoria, in the Fountains Valley Nature Reserve, a military stronghold built in 1898, commands strategic views of both Pretoria and the fertile countryside around. **Fort Klapperkop** has been spruced up and now serves as a museum of the military history of the *Zuid-Afrikaansche Republiek*, the Transvaal republic of the 19th century.

For miles around Pretoria, the hilltop **Voortrekker Monument** stands out. From afar it might be mistaken for an electric power station or some such windowless leviathan, but its purpose is purely symbolic – a shrine dedicated to the fortitude of the pioneers of the 1830s who trekked from the Cape to the Transvaal to perpetuate their language, religion and austere way of life.

An encircling wall is carved to represent a *laager*, the circle of ox wagons that the trekkers placed around their encampments to protect them against attack. Inside the granite monument a sculpted frieze commemorates incidents that took place during the treks. An aperture in the high-domed roof is placed so that at noon every 16 December a beam of sunlight penetrates to a crypt far below, illuminating the inscription on a sarcophagus, which reads: *Ons vir jou, Suid-Afrika* (We're for you, South Africa). The date is the anniversary of the Battle of Blood River, fought in 1838. Avenging the deaths of the Voortrekker leader Piet Retief and 70 of his men, the Boers killed about 3,000 Zulu warriors at a cost of only four wounded *(for visiting hours, see page 119).*

The monument's museum houses the **Voortrekker Tapestry**, a series of vivid needlework panels depicting events of the Great Trek. The museum also has dioramas that illustrate pioneer life; the typical Boer living room might be mistaken for an old Dutch farm scene were it not for the lion skin on the floor.

Forty kilometres (25 miles) east of Pretoria, at **Cullinan**, is the Premier Diamond Mine *(see page 120 for times of tours)*, a historic site in its own right: the 3,106-carat Cullinan diamond was unearthed here in 1905. From

Diversion: Sun City

The formerly austere restrictions of South Africa encouraged the creation of an escape valve in Sun City, in what was then the Republic of Bophuthatswana, only two or three hours' drive from Johannesburg and Pretoria.

Sun City is now part of the North West Province of South Africa. As you approach it rises like a mirage from the dusty bushveld. Outdoor facilities include golf courses, an artificial lake for waterskiing and parasailing and a well-stocked game reserve. The extraordinary Lost City theme resort is the biggest such project ever achieved in Africa.

The gambling scene at Sun City's entertainment complexes is a mini–Las Vegas. Slot machines pack mirrored halls. In the casinos roulette and blackjack cater to most punters (gamblers), with facilities for American craps, *chemin de fer* and *punto banco*.

Visitors come to Sun City by car, by tour bus, or by air to see the shows, uninhibited discotheques and blue films. Children are catered for with games and sports. Souvenir shops sell the handicrafts of the Tswana people and other African gifts.

Buses run frequently to Sun City from the Rotunda at Johannesburg's railway station and many tour companies operate excursions for a day, an evening, an overnight stay, or longer.

the fist-sized stone were hewn the Star of Africa and other gems now among the British Crown Jewels. The mine is still in business, producing about a million carats a year, though most of the stones are used for industrial purposes. Tour operators in Johannesburg and Pretoria run excursions to the mine, or you can go by car. The workings can be visited each weekday morning (you'll need strong shoes). Back in Johannesburg you can follow up the story by watching diamonds being cut and set into jewellery.

MPUMALANGA AND LIMPOPO

North of Pretoria, the sun-bleached highveld rolls on to a mighty escarpment, which plunges down to subtropical valleys below. This mountain region is one of South Africa's favourite holiday retreats, particularly as a stopover en route to or from the splendid game reserves of the north.

From Pretoria or Johannesburg to the **Kruger National Park** *(see pages 40)* is about 400km (248 miles) on excellent roads. The trip eastwards starts out through the grassy plains of the highveld, but less than halfway to Kruger Park the scenery undergoes sensational changes. One minute you think you could be in Scotland, the next the hills are as rugged as those in North Dakota, then suddenly the winding road plunges from cool spruce forests to banana plantations on the hot, humid lowveld.

If you're in a hurry, you can fly to Kruger Park or one of the private reserves. Travellers less worried about time can drive or take coach tours, going out and back on Route N4. If you have a day or two to spare, though, it's more interesting to take one route to the Kruger, travel through the park, leave by another gate and return to the Rand on a different road, taking in some of the following highlights of Mpumalanga and Limpopo provinces.

Nelspruit, on N4 and on the direct road and the Crocodile River, is the centre of a rich fruit-growing area which is surrounded by orange groves as well as orchards of mangoes, avocados and lichees. The town itself is handsome, with a population of more than 150,000.

In South Africa cars drive on the left, road signs are bilingual (English/Afrikaans).

An alternative route to the Kruger Park goes through the town of **Lydenburg**, where a few early buildings survive from the 1850s and over **Long Tom Pass** to **Sabie**, the site of a rich seam of gold, now worked out. Long Tom Pass is dramatically named after a gun used by the Boers against the British in 1900; the scenery is striking for its scale and emptiness.

Pilgrim's Rest, in a valley to the north, is well worth a diversion. Amid delightful pastoral scenery the heavily gouged hillsides give a clue to the past. A prospector named Alec 'Wheelbarrow' Patterson first panned gold here in 1873. News of the easy pickings spread quickly and Pilgrim's Rest took on all the trappings of a gold rush – 18 pubs could hardly cope with the crowds of miners. In the 20th century, as the mining technology became more and more sophisticated, the gold effectively ran out in 1972. When operations were closed down the provincial authorities bought up the town and preserved it as an oasis of nostalgia, with museums, gold-panning demonstrations, shops and hotels.

The forestry centre of nearby **Graskop** is a small town with mini-markets where you can replenish your picnic supplies. Past the regional centre of **Hazyview**, the road to the Kruger National Park is lined with menageries of animals – from pocket-sized specimens to giraffes.

If you can take a little more time, try to work out a route that allows you to see the **Blyde River Canyon**. 'Awe-

The Blyde River Canyon and its spectacular mountain views make this one of the most beautiful parts of the country.

inspiring' is no exaggeration for the views in this part of the world, where the Drakensberg mountains mark the transition from high veld to low. The geological surprises of the escarpment include rock faces of cliffs weirdly coloured by minerals, lichens and algae. The gorge itself is visible from many lookout points that are reached by long or short walks from the road. Three sandstone peaks – round outcrops topped by grass-covered cupolas – are called the **Three Rondavels**. Beyond them, **Mariepskop** is a mountain that has been squared off like an aircraft carrier. Hillsides plunge to the river as it zigzags through the creases, widening at last behind the Blyde River Dam.

Visitors to **God's Window** are rewarded by a panoramic view of the lowveld. Near Bourke's Luck, named after an old gold mine, the rivers Blyde ('joyful') and Treur ('sorrowful') converge in a three-way gorge. Three bridges made of aluminium offer views of this natural drama, from thundering waterfalls to **Bourke's Luck Potholes**, which seem to have been excavated by some gigantic ice-cream scoop. Displays at a visitor centre explain the local natural history. Accommodation is available at the **Aventura Blydepoort Resort**; tel: (013) 769-8005.

☞ KRUGER NATIONAL PARK

The first animal you will see in Kruger Park is not likely to be a lion or an elephant. It will more probably be a warthog scampering past with its tail standing up like a flagpole; or you may be delayed by the passage of a troop of baboons, the babies clinging upside down to their mothers' bellies. All this and a hundred prancing antelopes before you even reach your camp.

Warts and all: at Kruger National Park a muddy pool is often the location for a warthog family reunion.

There's no need to rough it here. Many 'huts' have air-conditioning, the shops are stocked to the ceiling and, if you are not cooking for yourself, a five-course dinner is served on white linen tablecloths in the restaurant.

Kruger National Park, about the size of Massachusetts, is South Africa's biggest wildlife sanctuary. It contains more species than any other game reserve on the continent of Africa, including several thousand elephant, about 25,000 buffalo, 120,000 impala and 30,000 zebra. And close to half a million humans are clocked in each year.

Accommodation may be reserved up to a year in advance through a travel agency or by writing to the National Parks Board, P.O. Box 787, Pretoria 0001. If you leave it to the last minute, you still stand a chance if you phone the reservation service at (012) 343-1991; e-mail; reservations@kruger-park.co.za. You could also check the park's website for information, <www.krugerpark.co.za>.

If no space is available, you might consider joining a package tour, as the tour operators make block bookings; or you could try to find accommodation in a hotel or camping ground outside the park but near enough for you to go in for day trips.

The range of accommodation inside the park should suit every kind of visitor, from the campers to the pampered. The simpler housing runs to thatched huts with or without showers and toilets. At the top of the scale are family cottages with kitchenettes and bathrooms with hot and cold running water.

Predicting the weather for the park is risky as it is so large, but the rainy season extends from September or October to March or April – mostly as brief thundershowers.

Before arriving in the area, don't forget to start taking anti-malaria pills, since both the Kruger Park and the private reserves alongside it are in a malaria zone *(see page 116)*.

The elegant impala can leap twice their height with ease.

The Camps

Of more than a dozen rest camps, most are in the southern half of the park, where the visitor traffic is concentrated. The biggest and best equipped are, from south to north:

Berg-en-dal. One of the newest camps, Berg-en-dal is attractively landscaped and includes the unusual luxury of a swimming pool.

Lower Sabie. Overlooking the Sabie River, situated very near the eastern edge of the park (the Mozambique border) and a short ride from its southern boundary.

Pretoriuskop. One of the earliest camps and the first to have a swimming pool.

Skukuza. More beds than any other camp and also more facilities, including a bank and post office, a car hire agency and a collection of more than 5,000 books about wildlife in English, Afrikaans, French and German.

Satara. Huts in a big circle around a pretty lawn and flower garden. Elephants come to drink at nearby dams.

Olifants. As the name suggests, this is elephant country. The camp enjoys a hilltop setting above the Olifants River, a haunt of hippos.

Letaba. The most centrally placed camp, near the Phalaborwa Gate, on a steep hill overlooking the Letaba River.

Shingwedzi. Another of the newer camps and one of three with a swimming pool.

Punda Maria. The most northerly of the camps, small and quiet, as relatively few visitors come to this area.

Each of the camps listed has its own restaurant, shop and petrol (gasoline) station as well as a variety of accommodation and a camping and caravan (trailer) site.

The Residents

Antelope. This is a generic term for animals as diverse as the wildebeest and the tiny steenbok. All males and some females have horns, some in dramatic shapes and sizes but never in the form of antlers. Of 19 species of antelope here, the most common are impala, elegant in their two-tone coats and able to leap twice their height with ease. (One species you won't see is the springbok, which is found mainly in the Kalahari region.)

Baboon. The dog-faced chacma baboon has a permanently worried look. Don't be tempted to offer them food; it's bad for their diet and personality and they could hurt you. Avoid them if you see them rummaging in dustbins at the camps. A troop of baboons is held in line by the big, dominant males, who grow to weigh nearly 41kg (90lbs) and can live to the age of 45.

Buffalo. Despite menacing horns, the Cape buffalo is peaceful enough – yet it can put up a fierce struggle with a lion. Since buffalo are steady drinkers, they like to stay close to waterholes or rivers. Buffalo are more active at night, preferring to play it cool when the sun shines.

Cheetah. This sleek cat is recognised by the marks that run from its eyes to the corners of its mouth, as if made by tears. The cheetah purrs but it cannot roar. It hunts its prey in broad daylight, reaching speeds of more than 100 km/h (62 mph) in short bursts.

Don't feed the baboons.
It's bad for their diet – and
their personality.

Elephant. The elephant population grows so rapidly that in the past several hundred were shot every year. When herds are too large, they strip forests bare, knocking down trees to get at the bark and drinking much-needed waterholes dry. Alternatives to culling, including a contraceptive vaccine, are being explored. Should your car become surrounded by meandering elephants, switch the engine off, keep quiet and wait for the herd to move along.

Giraffe. The stately walking skyscraper is not as easy to see or photograph as you'd think, as its blotchy coat blends in with the trees. It always seems to be munching leaves, which is why so many trees are trimmed into unlikely shapes. Giraffes are vulnerable to attack by lions – one reason they are reluctant to lie down; they sleep briefly, standing up.

Hippopotamus. The eyes and ears are what you're most likely to see, protruding from the surface of a river like the periscope of a submarine. Hippos are more comfortable afloat than on land, gravitating to water to keep cool, though at dusk and night they emerge on to dry land to graze.

Hyena. Skulking around with hunched shoulders and wailing that infamous laugh, the hyena is seemingly plagued by a guilty conscience – and an unflattering image. The alleged scavenger is a predator most of the time and a highly competitive one: the young actually attack each other from the moment of birth – they literally 'come out fighting'.

Leopard. As a nocturnal hunter, the leopard is hard to find. The best places to look are along rivers, among rocky out-crops, behind foliage, or up a tree. The leopard hauls its kill high into the branches, where most rivals can't reach it, so it can dine at leisure.

Lion. Safari photographers often have a problem getting shots of lions in action. The chances are the animals have dozed off, or they may be up to nothing more bloodcurdling than snuggling and playing together. Lionesses, which out-number the maned males, do most of the hunting, but a hun-gry male will drive off the rest of the group at feeding time.

Appetite for destruction: large herds of elephants are known for the havoc they wreak in the jungle.

Love of leaves – giraffes are hard to see, as they blend in with the trees whose leaves they like to munch.

Rhinoceros. A rhinoceros's long front horn is its weapon and threatens to be its downfall. Since powdered rhino horn is considered to be an aphrodisiac in Asia and parts of Africa – priced even higher per ounce than gold – poaching has all but wiped out the South African herds. To rectify the situation, hundreds have been reintroduced into Kruger Park. There are two species that are misleadingly named 'white' and 'black', though both look the same dirty colour after a good wallow in the mud. The so-called black, with its pointed mouth, is the more erratic and aggressive.

Zebra. A common but no less wondrous sight is a grazing herd of zebra, which number about 20,000 in the Kruger Park. The zebra feeds on grass alone, resulting in a great deal of migration in search of new fields. Highly strung and timid, zebra are likely to bolt at the first hint of danger.

When it come to **birds**, you'll be amazed at the variety that cross your path – long-tailed shrike or yellow-billed hornbill, bustards and the secretary bird – so named for the long feathers hanging from the back of its head like quill pens.

On the Lookout

Unless you pay attention you could spend hours roaming the park and see nothing wilder than antelope. Keep your eyes shifting from near to far, peering into the shadows, alert for any movement or discrepancy. Pay special attention to waterholes and, rivers, as the largest concentrations of animals are seen there and remember it's best to drive at well below the 50km/h (31mph) limit – especially on dirt roads, where there is more dust to stir up.

In the African summer the best times for spotting game are from sunrise to perhaps 11am and again in late afternoon in the hour before the park and camp gates close. In the cooler season the waterholes are active from predawn to noon and game can be seen at any time of day.

Wilderness Trails

Perhaps the irony has struck you: in game parks it's the humans who are confined – to camps and cars. In the Kruger, the way to escape this restriction is to join a Wilderness Trail group – eight hardy trekkers accompanied

Zebras are constantly on the look-out for the perils at large in Kruger National Park.

by an armed tracker and ranger. The trail followers, travelling on foot, stay out in the bush for three nights. Only small numbers of visitors (aged 12 to 60) can be accepted. Reservations can be made one year in advance, or you can always try for a last-minute cancellation; tel: (012) 347-0600 (SATOUR) for information.

 ## Private Game Parks

Another way to get close to nature – more comfortable but more expensive – is to book in at a private game park. Several operate in the bushveld along the western border of Kruger Park. Two- to five-day packages are offered, including flights from Johannesburg to the airstrips at Phalaborwa or Skukuza (or to one of the reserves that has its own).

In a private reserve, transport is by open Land Rover, with expert rangers and trackers as guides. Vehicles are linked by radio, so word can be spread when rare animals are seen. You can do more spotting in the productive hours around dawn and dusk than you can in the national parks, and night safaris with spotlights reveal the nocturnal creatures you might never otherwise see. By day, rangers and trackers lead walks, teaching you some of the secrets of the bush.

Luxury lodges such as **Mala Mala** and **Sabi Sabi** cosset their guests with the most attentive service and haute cuisine. Several other private establishments are somewhat less expensive but nevertheless provide expert rangers, air-conditioned accommodation, good food and swimming pools. Among a dozen or so in this group are **Thornybush, Londolozi and Inyati**. Information on the private reserves, as well as on national parks, is given in the *Where to Stay* guide published by the South African Tourism Board, SATOUR *(see pages 105 and 126)*.

KWAZULU-NATAL

KwaZulu-Natal province makes up only 8 percent of the nation's territory, but therein lies a remarkable geographical diversity, ranging from snow-prone mountains to a selection of beaches on the warm Indian Ocean. The people, too, range from Anglo to Zulu.

Vasco da Gama, the Portuguese navigator, first sighted these shores on Christmas Day in 1497 – hence the province's original name, 'Natal', Portuguese for Christmas. Following the political changes of April 1994 the province was renamed KwaZulu-Natal. Coastal Durban is its principal city.

The Natal Parks Board is responsible for about 50 reserves and parks, which it keeps as unspoiled as possible while providing comfortable cottages and chalets and plenty of attractive campgrounds. Some of the most impressive reserves are in the **Drakensberg Mountains** at the west along the frontier with the Kingdom of Lesotho. Stone Age Bushmen were attracted here because of the availability of small game and fresh water. They were driven out by a succession of tribes, most recently the Ngwaneni, who today live within sight of the Drakensberg peaks in their traditional wattle huts, shaped like haystacks.

A geological phenomenon known as the **Drakensberg Amphitheatre** constitutes the climax to the **Royal Natal National Park**. The panorama looks as if Mount Rushmore had been placed atop alpine foothills; the cliffs shoot down to steep green slopes. For mountain climbers, the highest peak, Mont-Aux-Sources, is a two-day undertaking: 3,282 metres (10,765ft) above sea level and 45km (28 miles) of difficult climbing, with some stupendous views as a reward. Mont-Aux-Sources is also accessible from the Free State if you go by Qwa Qwa.

The inhabitants of Royal Natal Park include several species of mountain antelope, as well as large colonies of baboons and dassies (rock-climbing mammals that look like oversized guinea pigs). Bird-watchers have counted nearly 200 species. For nature-lovers of all kinds there are hiking trails and easy walks through enthralling scenery.

The **Giant's Castle Game Reserve**, another Drakensberg wilderness, contains fantastic rock formations, along with caves and various treasures of Bushman rock art. The 'castle' itself, a few feet higher than Mont-Aux-Sources, is so awe-inspiring that the Africans called it 'The Mountain Not To Point At'. Wildlife includes eland (the biggest antelope) and a giant vulture, the lammergeyer. Storm clouds gather in these mountains on most summer afternoons.

Horse riders enjoy a trek through the lush valleys of the Drakensberg Mountains.

It's all downhill, slowly, from Giant's Castle to the coast. About halfway, at a refreshing altitude of 1,000 metres (3,280ft), is the resort centre of **Howick**. On the edge of town, the **waterfall**, plunging from street level into an abyss in the Umgeni Valley Nature Reserve, is a national monument.

Howick's waterfall is a national monument.

From here it's about 24km (15 miles) southeast to **Pietermaritzburg**, named after two leaders of the pioneer Voortrekkers, Piet Retief and Gerrit Maritz. The name is routinely shortened to Maritzburg. A city of parks and gardens with a population of about 200,000, it's at its best in spring when the azaleas are in bloom.

The founders of 1838 built wide streets and Cape Dutch houses, but their dreams of an unfettered Boer culture soon came to an end; the British occupied the town in 1842. Pioneer mementos – rifles, kitchen implements and a case full of *kappies* (bonnets) – are displayed in the **Voortrekker Museum**. A low building in Cape style which dates from 1840, it began its existence as the Church of the Vow, built after the Battle of Blood River. The oldest house in town has been moved to a site next to the Voortrekker Museum. This thatched, two-storey house, with its original tile floors and timbered ceilings, is now a small museum in its own right.

The fine Victorian **City Hall** (1893) is claimed to be the largest all-brick building south of the equator. Little shops and law offices line the narrow alleys nearby, whose names – like Chancery Lane and Gray's Inn Lane – evoke the Inns of Court of London. This area was the financial district, too, until the local stock exchange went out of business in the Depression year of 1931.

From Pietermaritzburg to the coast at Durban, the road, one of South Africa's super-highways, the subtropical countryside becomes ever more lush as the motorway descends. About halfway to the coast the motorway passes the **Valley of a Thousand Hills**, through which the short but powerful Umgeni River journeys to the Indian Ocean. This is the same river that was last seen taking a shortcut at Howick Falls. The thousand or so hills form an inspiring panorama.

If you would like to photograph tribal dances, make sure to ask for permission first.

This is Zulu country and one of the tourist attractions (coach parties go from Durban) is the **Phe-Zulu tribal kraal**, which calls itself a living museum; tel: (031) 777-1208. Each of the 'beehive' huts is designed to illustrate some aspect of tribal life. A highlight for visitors is the display of **dancing** to the rhythm of a drum and two-toned string instruments.

☞ DURBAN

They come from all parts of South Africa to hit the beaches and ride the surf or the roller coaster at Durban and, somehow, the town succeeds in combining the roles of brash beach resort and the busiest port in Africa.

Durban has come a long way since 1824, when a small British trading post was set up here to barter with the powerful Zulu nation. Originally called Port Natal, the settlement was renamed in 1835 in honour of the Governor of Cape Colony, General Sir Benjamin D'Urban. Despite many vicissitudes, Durban retains some aspects of England and the province of KwaZulu-Natal is the only one where the English language is more widely spoken than Afrikaans.

The personality of Durban is enlivened by its unique population mix: more than 500,000 Indian, 320,000 white and smaller numbers of black (mostly Zulu) and Coloured people. As everywhere else in South Africa, the races live to a great extent in separate areas, they are close enough together to promote something of a cosmopolitan air. Even the black townships are relatively handy to the centre of town.

Views over Durban and the resort of Umhlanga Rock.

For the tourist, the centre of Durban is the beach. Along the city's **Golden Mile** run four beaches – from south to north, Addington, South, North and Battery beaches. Formerly segregated, the beaches are now open to all races. Closest to the business district, South Beach is usually the most crowded. Ashore here are a children's amusement area, public bowling greens and the Seaworld aquarium and dolphinarium. **North Beach** is the hangout of surfers, thanks to the long, rolling waves and comfortable sea temperature along this stretch of coast.

Warm seas and rolling waves make North Beach a haven for surfers and swimmers.

On **Marine Parade** the last surviving rickshaws in Durban line up at a sort of taxi stand. The rickshaw was transplanted to Durban from Japan in Victorian times and quickly became a popular conveyance. Now only a handful are left, more for picture taking than for transport, pulled by Zulus wearing the most colourful tribal regalia. **Harbour tours** and deep-sea cruises depart from the Victoria Embankment, which faces south across Durban Bay. The bustling deepwater port – which handles three times the tonnage of Cape Town, South Africa's second-biggest port – makes for an interesting outing. Ships of many flags load and unload, while yachts and less grand pleasure craft come and go.

The business district is just a few steps inland from the Victoria Embankment. The **City Hall** (housing the Public Library, a good **Art Museum** and the **Natural Science Museum**) is said to be a copy of Belfast's – plus palm trees on either side of the portico. In nearby Smith Street the **Natal Playhouse** complex houses venues for the performing arts. At the **General Post Office** a plaque commemorates the arrival in Durban, just before Christmas 1899, of the young Winston Churchill after his escape from a Boer prisoner-of-war camp in Pretoria.

Durban's unique population mix lends the city a distinct cosmopolitan flavour.

Churchill's famous contemporary, Mohandas K. Gandhi, campaigner for Indian independence, first came to Durban in 1893 as a young lawyer and lived here on and off for 21 years, suffering many personal indignities because of his race. Gandhi conceived his philosophy of non-violent defiance in South Africa, where he led mass protests against discriminatory laws. He founded a farm collective near Phoenix, 18km (11 miles) north of Durban (leave the North Coast freeway at the KwaMashu exit). Much of the area is now a squatters' camp.

The heart of Durban's Indian business district, **Grey Street**, is a lively, exotic area to explore. Although only

Shark!

It takes only one headline — 'Shark Attacks Swimmer!' — to turn a prosperous resort into a deserted village, so it's vital to protect the beaches from the various deadly species that live in the Indian Ocean. The Natal Sharks Board catches more than 1,000 sharks a year just offshore. The board oversees more than 300 huge nets that essentially seal off 42 beaches.

Even so, the average beach in the province is closed 20 days a year. The most dangerous season is from June to August, when sardines migrate close to the shore, attracting so many sharks that the nets become clogged and damaged. If you see the 'no swimming' sign go up, believe it!

The board is supported by the provincial treasury and some money is earned from the sale of shark fins. There are tours on Tuesday, Wednesday and Thursday mornings.

In addition to sharks, scuba divers typically encounter a great number of less deadly species, including barracudas, sailfish, marlin, parrot fish, stingrays, dolphins and even whales.

The Western Cape whale route is active from June to September, affording visitors incredible views of migrating whales. The giant sea mammals have been known to pass so close to shore that onlookers sometimes get soaked by their mighty spray. One of the most popular spots for whale watching is at Hermanus, where a 'whale crier' blows a horn to alert spectators to whale sightings.

Water wildlife can also be observed farther inland. On Lake St Lucia boating tours bring passengers through the wetlands for close-up views of hippos, crocodiles and a seemingly endless variety of bird species.

about 20 percent of the local Indian population is Muslim, the Juma Mosque on Grey Street is reputed to be the biggest mosque in the southern hemisphere. Its arcades are occupied by shops selling a range of delicacies and jewellery, saris (spelt *sarries* in Durban) and European fashions. At the herbalist's, plants and roots hang from the ceiling.

At the vast **Indian Market** (officially the Victoria Street Market) nearby, Russell Street, offers a sample of the East. Engaging salesmen all but persuade you to buy enough 'hell-fire curry powder' for life. Also on sale are Hindu religious pictures and coral and wood carvings, many of them imported.

For a further feel of the tropics, try the Durban **Botanic Gardens** in Sydenham Road. In the orchid house there's a display of orchids, tropical ferns and vines. Outside, acres of lawns are shaded by an incredible variety of trees and elsewhere on the grounds there's a scent garden for the blind. Durban is proud of its parks, which include the formal **Japanese Gardens** and **Jameson Park**, where 200 varieties of roses bloom in springtime (September and October).

Golden beaches stretch in endless vistas north and south of Durban. To reach the south coast resorts you have to travel through the port and areas of heavy industry. Eventually, the scene improves as sweeping sugar lands come into view (some plantations and factories offer tours) and, finally, lush vegetation interspersed with uncrowded beaches.

Near Scottsburgh, **Crocworld** makes a nicely landscaped tourist attraction out of a commercial crocodile farm. The end of the line for the reptiles on view here is almost always the leather market.

North from Durban, the highway parallels the Indian Ocean between sugar plantations and the sea. The picturesque resort of **Umhlanga Rocks** (18km/11 miles from

Durban), with a lighthouse on the beach, is one place where the bathing should be safe – it is the home of the Natal Sharks Board.

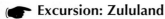

Excursion: Zululand

North of Durban, the part of KwaZulu-Natal still given the name of Zululand has some notable game reserves, as well as other attractions. The **St Lucia Reserves**, with a lake, estuary, dunes and beaches, offer wonderful wildlife with plenty of opportunities for bird-watching, snorkelling and scuba diving.

Inland, the varied rolling landscapes of **Hluhluwe**, one of the oldest game reserves in the country, and neighbouring **Umfolozi** are noted for both black and white rhino and a variety of other big game. To the north, **Mkuzi** is a newer game reserve that has become a favourite with bird-watchers. These and other reserves have camps with a range of facilities from tent sites to fully equipped chalets. The private lodges offer still more luxury.

About 14km (9 miles) north of Eshowe, **Shakaland** offers a 'kraal experience', a chance to enjoy a necessarily commercialised version of Zulu life for a day or overnight. You can stay in a hut (with modern plumbing) or a hotel, watch dances and displays and try Zulu cuisine.

Farther inland you can visit three **battlefields** of the 1879 Zulu War: Isandhlwana, where a British force was wiped out; Rorke's Drift, the famous site where a British garrison held out against the Zulus; and Ulundi, where the army of Ceteswayo was defeated. History buffs can spend weeks in the area tracing the sites where the Voortrekkers parlayed or fought with the Zulus and following the progress of the Anglo–Boer War from the British disasters of 1899 and 1900 through their laborious advance and on to their eventual victory.

From Durban, if you have the time to tour South Africa

by car, you can head south by way of the coastal resorts and then through Transkei to East London. From there a transit of the Ciskei region brings you to Grahamstown and Port Elizabeth. Some tour companies offer trips inland to visit game and nature reserves, where you can hunt, hike, or simply enjoy the wildlife. Alternatively, however, you can tour on your own; malarial precautions are necessary for some areas. For information, contact KwaZulu-Natal publicity offices *(see page 126)*.

PORT ELIZABETH TO CAPE TOWN

Shakaland offers visitors a commercialised version of Zulu culture.

South Africa's southern coast is a diverting and picturesque patchwork of beaches, forests and lakes. About a third of it is known as the Garden Route *(see page 61)*, but some extraordinary attractions can be found inland as well – including elephants and ostriches and the Cango Caves *(see page 67)*.

The country's motor industry is concentrated in **Port Elizabeth**, so maybe it's poetic justice that the very centre of the city should be violated by a network of super-highways on stilts, isolating the business district from the harbour. Fortunately, there is considerably more to Port Elizabeth than first meets the eye. For instance, there are the **beaches** fit for a king. At least, King's Beach – closest to the town centre – is where the British royal family took a dip during their 1947 tour of South Africa. Beyond, along Humewood Beach, an inviting mixed bag of the natural sciences can be viewed at the **Oceanarium complex**. The dolphin show here is outstanding, and the featured performers all originated in local waters.

Next door is the snake park, where a seemingly carefree handler wraps himself in puff adders, cobras and mambas while reciting a speech on the art of avoiding snakebites. Some 400 species of plants flourish in the sultry Tropical House. In the Night House (just inside the door of the Tropical House) the hours are reversed, allowing you to see nocturnal animals active in the dim artificial light.

> Most petrol stations are open from Monday to Saturday, 9am–7pm.

With a little imagination, you can picture Port Elizabeth as it must have been 60 years ago when the Campanile was built. The bell tower, 52 metres (171ft) tall and reminiscent of the one in Venice, rings out a 23-bell carillon concert every day at 8.32am and then at 1.32 and 6.02pm. You can climb it for a view over the city and harbour, but today the monument itself is almost invisible from the town, because of the motorway.

The **business district**, with big modern department stores, is what you'd expect in a city of more than half a million people. Main Street starts at the Mayor's Garden and the City Hall, a national monument dating from 1858. After a fire in 1977 the interior was re-done in a sparkling modern style, though no less stately than the building's exterior. A statue of Queen Victoria, facing the harbour, marks the main public library, in which you'll also find the local tourist office.

An hour's drive from Port Elizabeth, the descendants of the last elephants to live wild in Cape Province thrive in loose confinement in the **Addo Elephant National Park**. More than 100 animals roam a stockade large enough to give them elbow room but small enough to better your chances of seeing them. You might also glimpse black rhino, buffalo and several types of antelope. Restricting visibility, though, is the evergreen addo bush, which is short but impenetrable. Among all the tangled creepers are midget trees of

Addo elephant and calf, Addo Elephant National Park.

great beauty – wonderfully garish when in flower.

The Addo elephants won world attention in the 1920s. Stalking valuable farm land, they terrified local residents and damaged crops. A famous hunter, Major Pretorius, was contracted to exterminate the herd. In a period of almost a year, he killed 120, but 15 of the most cunning elephants eluded him. Public sympathy subsequently welled up for the victims and the survivors were thus reprieved. Setting up a national park for them was easier than confining them. Various types of fencing were tried and failed, until a high fence of tram rails and steel cables was devised. Eventually, it will enclose most of the park's 7,735 hectares (19,105 acres). Roads inside the enclosure pass near several waterholes where elephants are likely to appear in dry weather. Getting out of your car anywhere inside the stockade is forbidden. Another road along the outside has elevated viewing points.

The Garden Route

The N2 highway links Port Elizabeth and Cape Town. Exactly which stretch of this road deserves the semi-official title of the Garden Route is somewhat vague. The most attractive section runs about 220km (137 miles) between the mouth of the Storms River and Mossel Bay. But don't be misled by the name; composed of many kinds of countryside, often spectacular, the landscape of the route is not literally a garden.

West from Port Elizabeth, **Jeffrey's Bay** calls itself South Africa's surfing paradise – and indeed, the rollers here are well known to members of the international surfing set, who arrive in March for the start of the season. At any time of year the immense pink arc of sand is a delight – and a treasure trove of seashells, examples of which may be viewed in a **shell museum** in the library on the seafront.

In majestic countryside to the west, a splendid national park is centred near the Storms River. An ingenious and graceful bridge with a span of 192 metres (630ft) offers a formidable view down the gorge to the river far below. On the landward side of the N2 is the **Tsitsikama National Park**, with trees such as yellow wood, stinkwood and candlewood. Hiking trails are laid out to provide surveys of the big trees, the ferns and lichen, and the wild flowers.

Across the highway the park continues for about 80km (50 miles) along the rugged shore. The first coastal national park on the continent of Africa, it's a sanctuary for otter, bushback and vervet monkey, along with 210 species of birds. The restricted zone extends half a mile into the ocean, protecting dolphins, whales and the marine environment. A 41-km (25-mile) hiking trail, called the Otter Trail, follows the coastline over cliffs and through forests. You will also find yourself fording streams.

The Garden Route passes through some sensational scenery: there are endless stands of pine and eucalyptus behind roadside trees in blossom, tortuous stretches of road through and over gorges and sudden glimpses of the ocean from sheer cliffs.

The Garden Route takes you to Knysa, on the Western Cape.

When the Portuguese navigators of the 15th century saw **Plettenberg Bay** they were moved to call it Bahia Formosa (Beautiful Bay) – a judgement today's traveller would find hard to disagree with. The vast, classic arc of sandy beach is a favourite with visitors from far and near. The cape that protects the bay, called Robberg (Seal Mountain), supports a nature reserve that's accessible on foot.

On the way from Plettenberg Bay to Knysna you may be startled to see a sign pointing out the **Garden of Eden**. Here is a chance to stretch your legs and breathe the air of the primeval forest, where the sun's rays are barely able to filter through the interwoven branches of trees that were here long before the Portuguese first sighted the coast. The Forestry Department has labelled many of the garden's trees for educational purposes.

The 80,000 hectares (197,600 acres) of the Knysna forests are as valuable as they are beautiful. They were badly dimin-

Follow the scenic Garden Route for a myriad of spectacular coastal views.

ished in the 19th and early 20th centuries by reckless exploitation. With timber land constituting barely 1 percent of South Africa's total area, this resource is now necessarily carefully controlled by the government.

The town of Knysna (the 'K' is silent) is a popular resort that possesses an intriguing history. It was founded by a gentleman named George Rex, who was widely believed to be an illegitimate son of King George III of England. After arriving from the Cape at the beginning of the 19th century, he bought a big farm along the Knysna lagoon and turned the district into a seaport and a shipbuilding and timber centre. Boats and furniture are still made in Knysna, although the port lost its commercial importance with the arrival of the railway. Enthusiasts should make sure they do not miss the Outeniqua steam train, which still runs from Knysna to George *(see below)*.

The Heads, a famous rocky beauty spot, marks the dramatic entry of the Indian Ocean into Knysna's lagoon. The lagoon stretches far inland and provides ideal conditions for anglers and sailors alike. An unusual landmark along the lagoon is **Holy Trinity Church** at Belvidere, built in the 19th century along the lines of a Norman church. It's one of the smallest churches in South Africa, with enough room for only 65 people.

More lagoons and lakes, timber land and voluptuously moulded hills characterise the Garden Route west of Knysna. The next resort along the highway, **The Wilderness**, which offers hotels, camping sites and caravan (trailer) parks, is not as deserted as its name might suggest, but there are miles of unspoiled beaches.

George, the regional centre located at the intersection of the Garden Route and a main road to the Little Karoo, was named after George Rex's putative father, the king.

The most remarkable structure in this plateau town of 50,000 is an impressive **Dutch Reformed Church** – blindingly white and of dignified proportions.

The Little Karoo

In strangely beautiful semi-desert beyond the Outeniqua Mountains, about 56 km (35 miles) inland from George, **Oudtshoorn** is the capital of the Little Karoo. A stroll along any shopping street will soon show you what's different about this place. The stores sell ostrich feathers of many colours, empty ostrich eggs, dried ostrich meat, ostrich-hide wallets – even lamps and ashtrays standing on ostrich feet. Ostriches are big business in Oudtshoorn.

Off to the races – visit an ostrich ranch for ostrich-oriented souvenirs and fun.

The **ostrich ranches** on the outskirts of town offer an inimitable experience. In their thousands, nature's mightiest birds strut and scratch or stand about with vacant expressions in their bulging eyes. Guided tours of the farms cover the history of the Little Karoo's 90,000-strong herd, the boom of the Victorian era when ostrich feathers sold for 500 rand per kg (2.2lbs) and even tell you how to hatch an ostrich egg. There are ostrich races, in which the fleet, muscular, earth-bound bird have to run with 'jockeys' on their backs.

Why Oudtshoorn? It seems ostriches are happiest in a hot, dry climate; they like the type of alfalfa grown here and the availability of their favourite diet supplements – sand, stones and insects. In the same area other farms raise crocodiles for their skins and angora rabbits for their fur.

Twenty-six km (16 miles) north of Oudtshoorn, in the foothills of the Swartberg (Black Mountain), is another of South Africa's most popular attractions, the **Cango Caves**. They're easy to reach over a well-built mountain road that mostly follows a meandering river, its banks fringed by weeping willows. The caves once sheltered Bushmen, whose paintings were found on the entrance walls. Guides escort visitors into a series of chambers, pointing out the suggestive formations of stalactites and stalagmites. Modern amenities include refreshments and babysitters.

The last resort on the seaside section of the Garden Route is **Mossel Bay**, a working seaport with some beaches and natural swimming pools among the rocks. Although sailing ships visited the bay as early as 1488, the first permanent settlement wasn't established for almost 300 years. In the meantime, passing ships often stopped for water and to trade items with the local Hottentots. Sailors left messages to be relayed by other ships; the 'Post Office Tree', a big milkwood tree beside the freshwater spring, was the message centre. Some letters were stuffed into old boots and hung on it and the post office has put up a boot-shaped letter box next to the tree in the municipal park overlooking the beach. Mail posted there is franked with a special postmark.

The road to Cape Town heads away from the coast to **Swellendam**, one of the first inland towns in the Cape. It has a curious past, having declared independence from the Dutch East Indies Company in 1795, only to submit to the British the following year. Some fine buildings date from the 18th century and the wool boom of the 19th century. Close by, **Bontebok National Park** is home to the rare bontebok and other antelopes.

CAPE TOWN

One of the great experiences for any traveller is the first sight of Cape Town's classic combination of cloud-topped mountain, skyscrapered flatland and Atlantic Ocean.

Even though the climate suits pines, palms and frangipani, the locals complain. The winters aren't terribly cold but it does rain a lot. In summer a southeasterly wind as besetting as a curse assails the city for days at a time. They call it the Cape Doctor, for it is credited with sweeping away germs, mosquitoes and air pollution. During this season, too, Table Mountain acquires its distinctive 'tablecloth' – a strip of fluffy white cloud that hovers over the summit. The mountain itself is visible to ships as far as 160km (100 miles) off.

Cape Town's main street, **Adderley Street**, runs along the modern façade of the railway terminus. Between the station and the docks, the zone called the Foreshore has been reclaimed from the sea and is now occupied by an overpowering array of elevated highways and buildings that are designed to impress. The pedestrian mall on St George's Street hosts traditional marimba dance displays at lunchtime and on Saturday morning.

The giant **Civic Centre** straddling Hertzog Boulevard houses municipal officials and also the **Nico Malan Opera House and Theatre**, whose up-to-date technology behind the scenes can be seen on interesting guided tours.

The City Centre

Pedestrians make their way underground on the landward side of the railway station. In the passage beneath Strand Street the local tourist information office offers maps, brochures and accommodation advice. Also in the underground concourse is an old 'postal stone', under which 17th-century sailors placed letters to be picked up by homeward-bound ships.

Trafalgar Place, off Adderley Street, is the site of Cape Town's outdoor flower market, run by women of the Malay community. The Cape Malays are mostly the descendants of slaves brought from Southeast Asia in the late 17th century. They are Muslims and some still live in the **Malay Quarter**, or **Bo-Kaap**, near the business district (beyond Buitengracht Street). It's worth a visit to see the pastel-coloured houses, steep cobbled streets and minarets. Here you will also find the Jamai (or Queen Victoria) Mosque, Cape Town's oldest, dating back to 1850. Muslims of Indian extraction also live in this district, which survived the relocations of the apartheid era. Ironically, the character of the Malay Quarter is now threatened by the end of residence restrictions, as well-heeled outsiders try to buy up property here.

Most of Cape Town's inhabitants are Cape Coloured, that is, of mixed descent involving early white settlers, Hottentots and indigenous blacks or imported slaves. They outnumber the whites by nearly two to one. The black population of Cape Town is small, amounting to one out of every eight residents. Most of the blacks are Xhosa speakers; listen for the amazing clicking sounds in their conversation.

Cape Town **City Hall**, an Italian Renaissance-type palace from the early 20th century, faces the **Grand Parade**, which used to be a parade ground for troops. Before that the Dutch East Indies Company's first building in the Cape stood on this spot – an earthwork fort of 1652. Now the Parade is a big car park, relieved by a fruit and flower market and, every Wednesday and Saturday morning, a flea market. Beware of the pickpockets, who keep busy here.

Beyond the Grand Parade stands the **Castle of Good Hope**, reportedly the oldest building in South Africa, a sturdy, pentagon-shaped fortress that is now surrounded by a restored moat and inviting gardens. Guides lead tours of the castle several times a day, recounting its history, explaining the tactical layout and showing off the dungeons. The castle contains small military and maritime museums and also the William Fehr Collection of paintings, Cape silver and furniture and Asian porcelain.

Facing on to the cobbled **Greenmarket Square**, the **Old Town House** is a grand Baroque building dating from 1761 that served as the city hall until 1905. Now the white building with green shutters holds the Michaelis Collection of Dutch and Flemish art, including a treasured Frans Hals portrait and dozens of oils by his contemporaries. The **Groote Kerk** (Great Church), at the point where Adderley Street runs into pedestrianised Government Avenue, is sometimes called the oldest church in South Africa. Not much remains of the original Dutch Reformed church of the 17th century. The clock tower dates from 1703 and the rest was rebuilt much later.

Government Avenue, an oak-shaded gravel walk nearly a kilometre (more that half a mile) long, is a restful place to take a stroll in central Cape Town. It runs down the middle of the original Dutch East Indies Company's **Garden,** laid out by the first governor, Jan Van Riebeeck. Here, some 300 slaves produced fruit and vegetables for settlers and the visiting ships of the Company. About one-third of the original farm area has been turned into a resplendent botanical garden; the rest is occupied by buildings as important as the South African Houses of Parliament.

Several cultural institutions are sited around the Company's Garden, including the **South African National Gallery**, which highlights the work of South African artists and also has a strong showing of English painters.

The **Jewish Museum** nearby occupies the Greek-columned building of South Africa's first synagogue (1862); next door is the twin-towered Gardens Synagogue.

Dioramas of natural history and prehistoric life in Southern Africa, plus a valuable collection of Bushman rock paintings, are on show at the **South African Museum**, the oldest such institution in the country.

Cape Town's Castle of Good Hope is surrounded by inviting gardens and a restored moat.

Docks and Harbour

The port area starts close to the city centre, but it's so big you may want to explore it by car. Probably the best way to see the fleets of banana boats, fishing trawlers and container ships is on a harbour cruise or a trip round Table Bay.

The ambitious **Victoria and Albert Waterfront** development scheme for the two oldest dock basins has revitalised the area, creating a complex of restaurants, shops and entertainment centres, the South African Maritime Museum and a hotel in a former warehouse. The area has now become the Cape's biggest magnet for visitors, although it remains a busy working port.

☛ Table Mountain

People have been climbing Table Mountain since at least 1503, when the Portuguese mariner Antonio de Saldanha went up to check the lie of the land and sea. Today, climbers can choose from 350 routes to the 1,087-metre (3,565-ft) summit of the shale, sandstone and granite flattop. The climb can be dangerous, however, so amateurs are warned to start early, be certain of the weather and dress suitably (wear sensible shoes and carry some warm clothing, just in case). Guides are available to show you the way.

Alternatively, you can take the easy way – in seven minutes. The cable car has been whisking passengers to the top and down again, since 1929. There's plenty of room on top to roam, with maps and telescopes there. If the weather starts to deteriorate, a siren recalls visitors to the cable car station for a return to earth before service is suspended. In good weather, the cars operate half hourly from May to November from 8.30am to 6pm; from December to April from 8am to 10pm. If you're using public transport, take the city bus for 'Kloof Nek' from Adderley Street. A bus run by the Cableway

Company takes you on to the lower cable terminus.

For a spectacular picture of Table Mountain you may want to sign up for an aerial tour of the peninsula. Check with the tourist office, Captour, tel: (021) 418-5202. On land, northwards around Table Bay on the M14 highway, the road closes in on the sand dunes for a head-on view of the mighty cliff, with silhouettes of Devil's Peak and Lion's Head.

THE CAPE PENINSULA

Looking out from a viewing platform on Table Mountain.

The Cape of Good Hope is as gripping a part of the world as you'll ever see and the sights on the way are worth stopping for. There are two likely routes for exploring around the 50-km (31-mile) long peninsula. The more leisurely one starts out along the coast, counterclockwise from central Cape Town and the waterfront, passing South Africa's oldest working lighthouse at **Green Point**. Ferries make the 11½-km (7-mile) trip out to **Robben Island**, interesting for its flora and jackass penguins but famous for Nelson Mandela's imprisonment here. Groups are limited to 30 people, so bookings must be made in advance; tel: (021) 411-1006.

Sea Point is an in-town beach resort with a fashionable promenade and high-rent, high-rise buildings of every imaginable architectural style. For miles beyond, the road reveals beach after inviting beach alternating with rocky coves. Clifton Bay, with four beaches, is the most popular. The season is at its height from mid-October to mid-March. Along the Atlantic Coast, however, the water is cold all year round. For tolerable sea temperatures, go to the opposite shore of the peninsula and the warmer waters of False Bay.

The road soon turns inland along the slopes of the mountain formation known as the Twelve Apostles (actually a continuation of the back of Table Mountain). The highway returns to sea level at the big semi-circular fishing harbour of **Hout Bay**. Although some yachts are moored here, Hout Bay is obviously a working port. At certain times of the year the industrial aspects overwhelm the scenery, when factories producing fish meal and fish oil emit their vapours. Hout Bay is also an important source of a tasty South African delicacy, smoked *snoek* and the coveted crayfish (or rock lobster) and there are some good seafood restaurants.

A favourite excursion from here is by launch to some rocks known as **Duiker Island**, out beyond the calm of the harbour. Hundreds of seals can be seen diving and playing, the youngsters being cajoled into the sea to learn how to cope, the old-timers lolling on the rocks. Cormorants, gulls and oyster-catchers perch wing to wing on available spaces.

Continuing beyond Hout Bay, the Marine Drive rises to its climax – a corniche that hangs between cliffs and sea. When Chapman's Peak Drive was undertaken at the time of World War I, it was considered to be a breakthrough in road engineering. A lookout point is considerately provided at the highest spot on the drive.

The route soon swerves inland and crosses the Cape Peninsula, now hardly 10km (6 miles) wide. At the eastern extremity lies the small town of **Fish Hoek**, well known until recently as the country's only 'dry' community, as bars and liquor stores were forbidden here from the early 19th century until October 1994.

The other way from Cape Town to Fish Hoek is by the inland route. The M3 highway exits town as a busy but well-landscaped boulevard, passing the Groote Schuur Hospital. History was made here in 1967 when Professor Christian Barnard led the team that performed the first transplant of a human heart. Across the road, deer graze.

On the slopes of Devil's Peak, the **Rhodes Memorial** pays homage to the financier/statesman with an impressive monument: in a simulated Greek Temple at the top of a cascade of granite steps, a bust of Cecil Rhodes looks pensively out over what was his favourite panorama.

The oldest university in South Africa is set in priceless forested surroundings beneath Devil's Peak. The University of

Chapman's Peak Drive, a milestone in road engineering.

Seals on Duiker Island.

Cape Town, founded in 1829, has both traditional, ivy-covered buildings and stark modern ones, including the Baxter Theatre, which is an intellectual focus for the city as well as for the university.

About 3km (2 miles) past the UCT campus it's a short side trip off the M3 to **Kirstenbosch**, a renowned botanical garden. Thousands of species of plants grow here – representing nearly a quarter of all the types found in South Africa. (Because of the varied climates within the country no single botanical garden can cover the entire range.) August, September and early October are the most exciting times to visit here.

Cape Dutch Architecture

Dramatic landscaping adds to the visual impact of the old country seats of the Cape – big white houses, often thatch-roofed. Cape Dutch architecture is full of agreeable touches: symmetrical gables with curves and sometimes baroque intricacies; window shutters; wide main doors with fan-lights; and, inside, airy rooms with timbered ceilings.

One of the most magnificent Cape Dutch houses – **Groot Constantia**, south of Kirstenbosch – is now a museum. Great wines were produced on this farm from the turn of the 18th century. Part of the old cellars, behind the main house, has been turned into a wine museum. The main museum, which occupies the homestead itself, includes antique furniture, porcelain, implements and glassware.

Its name may make it sound like an imposter, but **False Bay** really is a bay, about 30km (19 miles) wide, with tantalising beaches. Returning from the Indian Ocean, some early navigators mistook it for the open Atlantic and made a hard right turn. Then they had to wait for a wind to extricate them. That's all that's false about False Bay.

A booming resort on this side of the coast, **Muizenberg**, first attracted attention in 1899 when Cecil Rhodes acquired a holiday cottage here. Now, thousands of visitors come from all over the country to wander across the endless dunes of almost snow-white sand. The sea here is quite good for swimming between November and April.

The suburban railway from Cape Town will take you to **Simonstown**, the main base of the South African navy. Ship spotters can see frigates and mine sweepers here and many an enviable yacht. A most unusual monument to Simonstown's past as a British naval base is a **Martello Tower**, somewhat hidden from view inside the dockyard area. This cylindrical stone fort, built in 1796, is thought to be the oldest of its kind in the world. It has been restored and now serves as a museum of naval mementoes.

In his search for the route to India, the Portuguese explorer Bartolomeu Dias rounded the Cape for the first time in 1488, although he couldn't see it for the storm that was raging. On his map he wrote, 'Cape of Storms'. On the return trip, Dias saw the Cape in the sunshine and renamed it the Cape of Good Hope. He was lost at sea in the same waters 12 years later.

Even though lighthouses, paved roads and a restaurant have been added, the **Cape of Good Hope Nature Reserve** remains virtually intact in its primeval state. Driving along

A beady-eyed ostrich.

the lesser roads you might come across eland, springbok, ostrich and other wildlife. Baboons, unfortunately, are legion. Signs in more than one language warn visitors that they face a nasty fine for feeding them (and if you leave your car, lock it up with the windows closed as baboons loot from unsecured vehicles). Specialists are fascinated by the flora – mostly low shrubs and grass. Everyone enjoys the outbursts of colour from wild protea and heather.

The reserve's long coastline varies from cliffs to rocky flats and sandy coves, but the high spot is where the roads run out, at **Cape Point**. A small bus called the Flying Dutchman shuttles visitors from the car park (parking lot) to the top of the final hill. From there you can walk to various observation points, the highest at the base of the original 1860 lighthouse. The new 19 million-candle lighthouse is purportedly the most powerful in the world.

At Cape Point, the granite cliffs plunge 259 metres (850 ft) to the sea – South Africa's tallest sea cliffs. Giant rollers boil and froth at the base, while cormorants fight the shrieking wind to reach their ledges. Albatross, gannets, gulls and giant petrels share the fishing in this tormented sea.

Looking west, you see the Cape of Good Hope itself, not actually Africa's southernmost tip – that honour belongs to Cape Agulhas near Bredasdorp – but still spectacular. The spot is accessible from the road, so you can climb the rocks near sea level for a close look at the breakers lashing the shore.

WINE COUNTRY

South African wines, which can hold their own against most competition, originate in a small corner of the country within a 162-km (100-mile) radius of Cape Town. The soils and microclimates within this arc are so varied that all manner of wines can be produced, from sweet and dry whites to rosés, reds and fortified types in the style of sherry and port.

One-day excursions offered by tour operators cover two principal centres, Stellenbosch and Paarl – or you can do the trip on your own at a more leisurely pace and take in some other stops as well. The tourist information offices of both regions issue maps and brochures and will also suggest itineraries. The scenery itself is enchanting.

Dutch colonial style is a common feature among the houses of Stellenbosch.

Stellenbosch, under 50 km (31 miles) east of central Cape Town, has more beautiful old buildings than any other municipality in South Africa. It's an endearing, relaxed university town named after that great 17th-century wine enthusiast, Governor Van der Stel. Fires destroyed the original thatched cottages and the best of the buildings on view today date from between 1775 and 1820. They're all different, but harmonious: on the same scale, white-washed and delightful.

The Cape of Good Hope is not actually the southernmost point of Africa but it's still a breathtaking sight to behold.

Grosvenor House, an early-19th-century mansion with an award-winning garden, is filled with authentic Old Cape furnishings. **Schreuder House** (1709), with simple settlers' furnishings, is possibly the oldest surviving town house in South Africa.

A homestead of 1780 houses the **Rembrandt Van Rijn Art Gallery**. In the same compound a wine museum displays old Roman amphoras and antique glasses and bottles. Nearby is a museum featuring the history and technology of brandy-making.

Around Stellenbosch, vineyards spread for miles over hillsides and flat land, imparting something of a Mediterranean feel to the area, while imposing mountains form a backdrop. About 15 **wine estates** and cooperatives in the district welcome visitors daily except Saturday afternoon and Sunday, usually offering scheduled cellar tours, wine tastings and, of course, opportunities to buy. Look for the 'Wine Route' logo on the estate signage.

The Cape's other main wine region centres on **Paarl**, about 60km (37 miles) from Cape Town, just off the N1 motorway. It's about twice the size of Stellenbosch, with a huge modern civic centre that also houses the information office. Paarl, however, is an old town with a winning atmosphere. The seemingly endless main street is lined with historic buildings, working vineyards and the headquarters of KWV, the Cooperative Wine Growers Association. Tours are scheduled four times a day.

The **Old Parsonage (Oude Pastorie) Museum**, in a perfectly restored, 18th-century Cape Dutch building, has a fine collection of old Cape furniture and silver.

Elsewhere in Paarl and the surrounding Berg River Valley are half a dozen **wine estates** and 10 cooperative cellars. Most have wines for sale, with or without tastings, and cellar tours either on a schedule or by arrangement.

An excellent view of the town, vineyards and nearby mountains is afforded from the site of the **Taalmonument**, a monument to the Afrikaans language set high on a hilltop above the southern outskirts. From a distance the monument looks like a family of stalagmites; close up, it's a complex work of abstract art. The idea of honouring a language in such a way is somewhat unusual, but Afrikaans-speakers cling to theirs with a fierce pride.

The more time you have, the more treasures you will be able to discover in this part of the Cape. **Ceres**, a pretty town at the heart of a rich fruit-growing region, is well worth a visit; and **Tulbagh**, which dates from the early 18th century, has some of the most beautiful Cape Dutch houses of all (now carefully restored after damaged caused by an earthquake in 1969).

In South African wine country there are some 15 wine estates and cooperatives that welcome visitors for tours and tastings.

CAPE TOWN TO JOHANNESBURG

You can fly back to Johannesburg, of course, but if you have time you'll see more of the country by driving or taking the train. For train travellers the choice is between the regular service and the luxury Blue Train *(see box opposite)*.

The railway and the direct road both cross the vastness of the semi-desert, **Great Karoo**. Despite its lack of rainfall, some fascinating specialised forms of plant life are able to flourish in the desert and in places water is pumped up from bore holes to sustain the flocks of sheep. If you're travelling by car, **Kimberley** makes a convenient overnight stop and you can take the opportunity to see the famous 'Big Hole'. About 1½km (1 mile) round and half as deep, the excavation at the top of this 'pipe' from the depths of the earth was the source of over 14 million carats of diamonds between 1871 and 1914.

It looks a long way on the map, but the good roads and light traffic mean that the journey from the Cape to Johannesburg is an easy two-day trip. An alternative to the shortest route involves only a couple of hours' more driving. It heads north up the western Cape through lovely scenery (and in September,

The Blue Train

The 1,608-km (997-mile), 26-hour journey by the Blue Train between Cape Town and Pretoria via Johannesburg is one of the world's most luxurious. A five-star hotel on wheels, it offers three-room suites – lounge, bedroom and bathroom with a real bath – or simpler quarters, all enjoying that air-conditioned sense of well-being. The designers thought of everything: a thin layer of gold on the double windows reduces heat and glare; venetian blinds between the panes operate electrically; and air springs guarantee a quiet, smooth ride.

The party starts out glamorously with free bubbly for brief on-board going-away parties. After the last-minute excitement, flags wave and the 16-car train eases into motion. The journey is not about exerting yourself and all you need do is lounge in the bar, eat the many-coursed meals (food is included in the ticket price), read and watch the passing scenery. Table Mountain and the Cape vineyards gradually give way to the semi-desert of the Great Karoo. The approach to Johannesburg is indicated by the truncated pyramids of gold-mine waste heaps.

Reservations for the Blue Train (tel: (011) 774-4469, fax: (011) 773-7643) are taken 11 months in advance.

For international calls from South Africa you must first dial 091.

spectacular wild flowers) to **Springbok**, then east via **Upington**. A short diversion will give you a chance to see the **Augrabies Falls**, where the Orange River thunders over the escarpment, forming one of the world's great waterfalls.

Having come so far, those with an adventurous bent will be tempted by the chance to see South Africa's strangest extremity, its piece of the Kalahari Desert. A tongue of territory jutting out between Namibia and Botswana, the **Kgalagadi Transfrontier Park** is reached by dusty but well-graded roads. The park has excellent accommodation and other facilities. While here, you'll see not only the handsome gemsbok, but also springbok, lion and, if fortune favours you, cheetah as well.

Spring flowers in Namaqualand offer spectacularly colourful views to visitors.

WHAT TO DO

SPORTS

South Africans are dedicated to the outdoor life. Half the country seems to be wielding fishing rods or golf clubs, running, swimming, or riding surfboards. The other half is likely to be watching cricket, rugby, football, wrestling, or racing. In general, sporting stars tend to receive more publicity and acclaim than mere film celebrities or politicians. SA-TOUR and CATASA (Council of Adventure Travel Agents of Southern Africa, tel: 0140-892-417) can provide useful information about sporting activities and tour operations.

Watersports

South Africa's 3,000km (1,860 miles) of beaches cater for all tastes. In parts of KwaZulu-Natal and the Cape, dunes stretch endlessly into total wilderness. If you prefer convenience and crowds, the popular resorts have all the facilities. Because of sharks and tricky tides, swim only where signs indicate it's safe. The busier beaches have lifeguards on duty. If the waves are too high or the sea is uncomfortably cold (as it can be at the Cape), you can fall back on the hotel swimming pool.

Watersports at Fish Hoek.

Surfing has become a South African passion. The waves of the eastern Cape are fit for champions, with often impeccable conditions to be found at Cape St Francis and Jeffrey's Bay, and warmer waters in the Durban area. For information, contact the South Africa Surfing Association, tel: (0391) 21150.

Windsurfing (boardsailing) is the fastest-growing watersport in South Africa, from the Indian Ocean to the chilly Atlantic (where wet-suits are standard) and on lakes inland. Check with the South African Windsurfing Class Association (tel: (011) 726-7076) for those areas that require permits for offshore windsurfing. Old-fashioned sailing hasn't lost its allure, with dozens of yacht clubs offering facilities and classes at all levels. The Cruising Association of South Africa can help with specifics, tel: (021) 439-1147.

For still more varied thrills, two-day **white-water rafting** trips are offered on the rivers of the Cedarberg north of Cape Town (look in the 'What's On' type of free magazine or check with travel agents). You'll find **scubadiving** schools and clubs in the vicinity of all the main coastal resorts. Contact the South African Underwater Union, tel: (021) 930-6549.

Fishing

Whether they prefer rock, surf, or deep-sea fishing, anglers have a field day in South Africa. Everything they could dream of can be found in the South Atlantic and Indian oceans. The oceans' meeting point, near Cape Town, is said to be the home of more kinds of game fish than any other sea; for instance, in the past all species of marlin and tunny (tuna) have been landed here. In the big ports, such as Cape Town and Durban, you can take part in organised **deep-sea excursions**. Elsewhere, small, powerful ski boats may be hired to reach the action.

The best seasons for rock and surf fishing vary with the region. In the southwestern Cape, it's January to April, but along the KwaZulu-Natal coast the most promising time is June to November. There is unparalleled excitement in June between Port St Johns and Durban: immense shoals of sardines run along the coast, attracting shark, barracuda, kingfish and shad, which in turn lure anglers to the scene. If you want to join the crayfish (rock lobster) hunt, you will need a licence, and there are seasonal restrictions for these and for oysters and abalone (here called *perlemoen*).

Inland, rivers and lakes all over the country offer the chance to fish for trout, bass, and carp. There are strict catch limits in most places and permits are required; contact the local parks board or Department of Nature conservation for permit and catch requirements.

Sports on Land

Golf has been played in South Africa for well over a century and there are courses of international repute to be enjoyed here. Hundreds of courses welcome visitors, at least on weekdays, when even the public courses are not normally overcrowded.

Horse-riding on the Eastern Cape.

You are advised to contact club secretaries for start times and to check dress codes. The South African Golf Development Board can also advise; tel (021) 852-8056. Golf is played all the year round, but over most of the country the greens are at their greenest in southern summer (December to March). Carry an umbrella for those inevitable afternoon rainstorms.

The good weather makes year-round **tennis** a possibility, too. The equivalent of Wimbledon in South Africa, Ellis Park in Johannesburg boasts 21 tennis courts. The Wanderers is one of more than 170 tennis clubs in the city and has 26 courts. Most of the resort hotels either have their own courts or else have access to facilities nearby; for more information call the South African Tennis Union, tel: (011) 402-3580. In addition, some of the hotels also have **squash** courts.

The tranquil-looking, but nevertheless highly competitive, British game of **bowls** arrived early in South Africa, spreading from Port Elizabeth to KwaZulu-Natal and the Rand. Today 60,000 bowlers belong to some 800 clubs; visiting players from abroad are welcomed.

Horse riding and associated sports take place all over the republic. The Johannesburg area alone numbers 20 riding schools, and out in the wilds some country hotels have their own stables. Pony treks are arranged by the Natal Parks Board (tel: 0331-47-1981) in the Drakensberg mountains.

A series of **hiking** trails is being developed which will eventually reach from the mountains of the Cape to the northern Transvaal. Information and addresses to write to for maps and details of individual trails are contained in the booklet *Follow the Footprints*, which is available from SA-TOUR *(see Tourist Information Offices, page 126)*.

Horse racing takes place year-round at tracks in all the major cities. The race of the year is the Durban July Handicap, which is run on the first Saturday of July. The Metropolitan Stakes, held at Kenilworth Race Course in Cape Town, is an important social event usually held in January.

The **motor racing** circuit at Kyalami, north of Johannesburg, hosts a range of motor and motorbike racing events throughout the year.

Rugby, **cricket**, and **football** (soccer) have practically attained religious status among participants and spectators alike. Although efforts are being made to provide black South Africans with better playing facilities, rugby is still a predominantly white pursuit. You can see top-class matches at the huge Ellis Park stadium in Johannesburg, at Newlands in Cape Town, and indeed in every city and town throughout the winter. Other popular **spectator sports** include boxing, wrestling, and athletics.

It's quite costly, but you can go **hot-air ballooning** in the Magaliesberg near Johannesburg or in the KwaZulu-Natal Drakensberg, where you'll also see hang gliders doing their stuff. In fact, if any form of sport or exercise catches on anywhere in the world, you can be sure that it will soon find popularity in South Africa.

Adventurous types can try hot-air ballooning at Magaliesburg.

The successful conservation of the game herds means that for some species there has to be a culling programme, and this opens up the possibility of **hunting**. Details of quotas and costs and other information can be obtained from SA-TOUR *(see page 127)*.

A growing interest in the **martial arts** has an obvious link with self-defence in the city streets. **Mountain biking** has become as much a passion with the young as it has in many Western countries, but a game called **jukskei** seems to be home-grown: in the same way that Americans throw horse-shoes, Afrikaners have taken to throwing sticks.

Saturday is the most important day of the week for organised sports in South Africa. While for many years sporting activities of any importance were banned on Sundays, breaches of this taboo are now routine and games are played regularly.

SHOPPING

South Africa's shops are remarkably diverse – from stalls at flea markets and quaint bazaars to air-conditioned boutiques and big-city shopping centres vast enough for hours of browsing. The odd sign in a shop door, 'Closed Owing to Weather. Come In' means the door, not the shop, is closed to wind or rain.

Visitors buying more expensive items, or a lot of smaller ones, can reclaim the value-added tax (VAT.) at their point of departure from the country. To do so they must show the items concerned as well as proper VAT receipts.

What to Buy

African curios. There's no end to the supply of tribal shields, spears, and masks, which are mostly produced by the manual equivalent of assembly lines. Some of the more artistic designs and older items come from other countries, in particular Zaire.

Beads. Early traders from Europe brought glass beads to exchange for ivory or other valuable commodities. Now European tourists buy beadwork necklaces, dolls, and ornaments in various bright geometric designs.

Butterfly pictures. Each picture comes with an assurance that no butterfly has suffered in the course of its creation; tiny parts of wings of different colours are assiduously glued together to form a coherent African scene.

Chess sets. Figurines of African warriors represent the pawns, medicine men the bishops, and so on.

Diamonds. This is their country of origin, so you might consider picking up a bauble. Jewellers licensed by the South African customs give duty-free prefer-

Original pieces of jewellery are abundant in South African outdoor markets.

ence to bona-fide foreign visitors on diamonds that are cut, ground, and polished but not set. Semi-precious stones, which also abound here, come closer to most budgets: these include agate, amethyst, jasper, rose quartz and verdite.

Flowers. South Africa's national flower, the protea, may be carried home, dried, and boxed with pampas grass and other typical flora.

Straw goods such as baskets, hats and bags are a mainstay of South African crafts.

Indian spices. Curry powders and chilli peppers with explosive colours and flavours are likely souvenirs of Durban.

Jewellery. Certain jewellers with special customs licences are able to sell gold pendants, chains and earrings to visitors without charging the stiff levels of South African duty. You will have to show your passport, air ticket and flight reservation to qualify.

Krugerrands. Collectors of gold will always be pleased to receive one, or a set, of these desirable and portable South African coins. They may be purchased duty-free for foreign currency in the departure lounge of Johannesburg's Jan Smuts Airport.

Musical instruments. You will soon learn to play one of those small bush xylophones of metal spikes and carved wooden base. You can also take home a small drum-rattle or a big carved drum to thump.

Ostrich eggs. Gaily painted or *au naturel*, these jumbo-sized eggs are definite conversation starters. More useful are ostrich-skin wallets and handbags.

Pottery. African artisans produce coiled pots with ancient tribal designs or thrown pots with new, original motifs.

Rugs and tapestries. Handwoven in geometric or figurative designs, these are suitable for wall-hangings or carpets. From spinning wheel to final trimming, some of these works of rural art are produced with meticulous care.

Seashells and coral. Those vast beaches turn up seashells which serious collectors covet. Coral fantasies, although controversial, are sold in curio shops on the coast and inland.

Straw goods. Bags, baskets, hats, mats and trays are sold in souvenir shops or by the roadside at makeshift stalls.

Wines. Quality wines and local versions of sherries, ports and brandies make natural souvenirs of the Cape.

Woodcraft. Salad bowls, meat trays, spoons and ladles are readily available. Wooden sculptures run from miniature rhinos to large, elaborate carvings incorporating entire tribes of figures. The fine-grained local hardwoods make solid furniture and fine carvings. Don't be put off by the name given to stinkwood – it only smells when freshly cut.

Zebra skins. Stripes for your wall or floor reach reputable shops from authorised game-park sources. Much less expensive are the antelope skins, out of which items such as handbags, cushion covers, and wallets are made.

Most countries now ban imports of ivory; this ban also applies to elephant tusks that have been obtained legitimately from the culled herds of the Kruger Park.

Durban's large Indian population is the source of a vast array of spices.

ENTERTAINMENT

The big cities, townships, and resort towns have **nightclubs** and a lively nightlife, mostly in or near the major hotels. In Johannesburg the Rockey Street area is the popular place to go for live music, restaurants, and clubs. This can be a seedy area, so avoid wearing conspicuous jewellery and carrying large amounts of cash. For details of the latest venues, live music performances, and other current events, consult the local press or tourist board publications such as *Hello Johannesburg*, *Hello Cape Town*, or *Time Out*.

Bars remain closed on Sundays. Some restaurants are licensed to serve alcohol.

Regulations governing alcohol are complex. For instance, while bars are closed on Sundays, licensed restaurants can serve beer or wine with meals. Bars are relatively few and usually quite rudimentary, except in hotels. 'Ladies' Bars' are actually intended for men and women who are together.

In the major cities, lively professional **theatres** present plays in either English or Afrikaans. Some of the most important include the State Theatre in Pretoria, Johannesburg's Civic Theatre and Cape Town's Baxter Theatre. The National Symphony Orchestra performs in the major centres and there are a number of accomplished opera and ballet companies.

Cinemas show current international film releases, and censorship has been greatly relaxed. There are several performances daily and advance booking is available.

In cities including Johannesburg, Pretoria, Cape Town and Durban, tickets to films, plays, and concerts may be bought at branches of *Computicket*, a computerised booking agency. Consult the local papers for current information on performances.

EATING OUT

With 13 million head of cattle on South African prairies and two oceans to provide the fish, you're assured of good food in abundance. Cooking here has the old-fashioned virtues – it's wholesome and there's plenty of it. You may indeed be daunted by the sizes of the portions. In many restaurants 'doggy bags' are called for, in the American way, so that the excess can be taken home

City restaurants come in all varieties, from five-star haute cuisine and elegance down to the most utilitarian fast-food joint. Italian, French and Chinese cuisines abound, but Johannesburg claims ethnic restaurants of 20 nationalities, including Japanese, Korean, Greek, Indonesian, Turkish and Mexican. Many Cape restaurants serve old Cape Dutch and Malay recipes. Durban is noted for its Indian restaurants, and offers the cuisines of various region of that continent.

Fisherman unloading the catch of the day in Durban.

Outlets calling themselves cafés are not what the rest of the world means by that name. You can buy take-away (take-out) food and soft drinks in a South African café, but there's nowhere to sit down and have a coffee or tea, much less an actual meal.

In all hotels except, paradoxically, the most expensive, breakfast will normally be included in the price. Even if it isn't, it's likely to be good value, typically consisting of fresh fruit and juice, hot or cold cereals, kippers or smoked haddock, bacon or sausage, eggs, toast and rolls, butter and marmalade and tea or coffee. Many hotels have breakfast buffets in the Scandinavian manner, though the dishes on offer are more British in derivation, as is the morning 'wake-up' coffee or tea that you can have brought to your room.

At the game lodges it makes sense to take that coffee or tea at dawn or before, then go out looking for the wildlife prior to returning for a hearty mid-morning breakfast.

Fish and Seafood

All along the coasts you'll find fish restaurants that clearly have good connections down at the harbour, but most restaurants, specialist or not, have fish on the menu, usually fresh. Cape salmon is a tasty white fish, unrelated to the salmon of Europe and North America. *Kabeljou* is similar to cod. *Kingklip*, a large meaty fish, makes fine fillets. *Snoek,* a cold-water fish about a yard long, is served smoked as a starter or grilled as a main course, while *Steenbras* resembles sea bream.

The excellent shellfish is worth seeking out: mussels, *perlemoen* (abalone), prawns (the latter often imported from Australia). The local crayfish (elsewhere called spiny rock lobster) is a delicacy. Oysters may be served with hot sauce already applied – remember to specify in advance if you want yours unadulterated.

Meat

South Africa's favourite food is *braaivleis* (barbecued meat), a feast cooked in the garden or at a picnic spot. Men are generally in charge and the whole business is taken very seriously: special cuts of meat are sold for the purpose, and hardwood is selected for its proper fire-making qualities.

You may be invited to a **braai**, or you can buy the meats and the wood and use the barbecue you'll find outside most chalets or rondavels in game park camps. Otherwise, the many steak houses serve a pretty good approximation of the outdoor taste. The steaks – fillet, rump, sirloin, tournedos, or T-bone – are invariably big, thick and tender. Whether you ask for it or not, the cook is liable to grill them with a barbecue sauce. A number of other sauces are usually on the menu, the most piquant being 'monkey gland' sauce (hot sauce and chutney).

In steak houses and other restaurants you'll also find a variety of alternatives: lamb, veal, pork, poultry,' and game. All dishes

Braaivleis – delicious outdoor cooking.

come with potatoes (usually chips – French fries – or baked) or, less commonly, rice and cooked vegetables — beans, broccoli, carrots, mushrooms, pumpkin, squash, sweet potatoes or *mealies* (corn on the cob). Steak houses and some other restaurants may have salad bars in the American style – a big choice of nutritious raw vegetables and dressings to mix and match.

Local Favourites

Don't miss the traditional South African meat dishes, particularly *bobotie*, a baked minced-meat recipe from the Cape. It's probably of Malay origin, with its additions of apricot, almond, chutney, and a subtle spicing of curry. *Boerewors* are flavourful country sausages, usually of a beef and pork combination. *Bredie* is a rich ragout, usually of mutton, with a thick tomato sauce. *Sosaties* are kebabs, resembling Southeast Asia's *satés*, little pieces of lamb marinated in vinegar, sugar, garlic, curry powder and apricot. Varieties of smoked pork are another local speciality.

Biltong, strips of dried meat, was once made out of necessity, to take on treks and for preserving surplus meat before the days of refrigeration. Now it's something of a delicacy and comes in many varieties (made from anything from impala to ostrich).

Desserts

If you still have space, there may be apple pie, *melktert* (minimal pastry and a light, gently spiced custard), cheesecake, or trifle in the English style (sponge cake smothered in fruits, nuts, custard and whipped cream). Then, of course, there's always fresh fruit – small, sweet pineapples, bananas of various kinds, melons, apples, grapes, and *naartjies* (mandarin oranges). Also, look for home-made ice-cream of real fruit flavours.

Excellent South African versions of many European **cheeses** – brie, camembert, cheddar, gouda, mozzarella and so on – are hardly distinguishable from the originals, except that the price is lower.

Before you've finished your dessert the waiter may present you with the bill. This is not intended to hurry you out. Nevertheless, it is rare for South Africans to linger at the table after a meal.

Wines and Other Drinks

Cape wines have come a long way. The early settlers grew the classic grape varieties, but the same plague that ravaged the vines in Europe in the 1880s struck South Africa, and the country's vineyards had to be replanted with resistant American grafts.

The grapes are still mostly familiar: Riesling, Chardonnay, Sylvaner among the whites, and Cabernet Sauvignon, Pinot Noir, Gamay and Merlot for the reds. In addition, there are two native South African varieties: Steen is a general-purpose grape used to make sweet and medium-dry white, rosé, and Champagne-style wines. The other is called Pinotage, a cross between Pinot Noir and Hermitage (Cinsaut), which makes full red wines.

Aside from wine, there are European-style beers (served very cold), well-known brands of soft drinks (called cool drinks) and mineral waters. Fruit juices, freshly squeezed or pasteurised, are delicious. Look out for some of the exotic mixtures: guava, lime, mango, apricot, peach and pear. You won't cause any surprise by asking for tap water, which is drinkable everywhere.

Note: Many restaurants lack wine or liquor licences, so it is wise to check in advance. South Africans often bring their own wine to licence-less restaurants If you don't, it's no good expecting to go to a nearby wine shop: they open only during normal shopping hours and never on Sunday.

HANDY TRAVEL TIPS

An A–Z Summary of Practical Information

A

ACCOMMODATION (See also CAMPING AND CARAVANNING on page 102, YOUTH HOSTELS on page 124 and the selection of RECOMMENDED HOTELS starting on page 125)

The South African Tourism Board (SATOUR) publishes an annual directory of hotels with ratings – five stars for the pinnacle of luxury, one star for simple comforts. At the top level you can expect a swimming pool, tennis courts, sauna, choice of restaurants and bars and air-conditioning throughout. The prices match the standards, but the degree of comfort of hotels at the lower end of the scale is also notable. Many two-star establishments, for instance, have spacious air-conditioned rooms, and one-star hotels have a high percentage of rooms with private baths. In hotels rated by the board you are generally assured of good value for money.

SATOUR'S directory also includes luxury lodges and rest camps in game parks, beach cottages and holiday flats for the whole country. There is a separate guide to caravan (trailer) and camp sites. Both directories can be obtained from SATOUR'S national and international offices; they are invaluable for planning ahead, for use on arrival, and while you're touring. Accommodation is normally heavily booked for the South African school holiday periods (December–January, Easter, June–July and early October), but at other times there should be no problem. On the contrary, off-season reduced prices may apply.

Among many other details, the hotel directory reports the status of every establishment's liquor licence (if any), its policy on pets, whether there is wheelchair access, and gives an indication of price which, because of inflation, may be outdated. Prices include Value-Added Tax (VAT) at the standard rate.

South Africa

AIRPORTS

South Africa's principal airport, Johannesburg International Airport, is about 24km (15 miles) from Johannesburg and 60km (37 miles) from Pretoria. Services in the terminal include restaurants and bars, shops, hairdresser, pharmacy, florist, post office, bank, insurance and car-hire (rental) desks and duty-free shops. For airport enquiries telephone (011) 970-1669.

Metered taxis are available. An airport bus runs to and from the South African Airways (SAA) terminal (called the Rotunda) opposite Johannesburg's main railway station, leaving every 30 minutes from 5am to 10pm. The trip takes about half an hour. For enquiries to the SAA. terminal telephone (0860) 359-722.

Another bus service links the airport and Sandton City, and there is also a service to and from Pretoria (leaving the city SAA terminal about two hours before flight departure).

Other international airports are at Durban and Cape Town. Durban Airport is 16km (10 miles) southwest of the city, and is served by a bus service to the SAA town terminal; Cape Town Airport is 22km (14 miles) southeast of the city, and a bus service runs to the railway station.

Domestic routes flown by South African Airways and a number of small independent airlines link the main cities and some smaller centres. Various private airlines operate flights to other towns and to Skukuza and Phalaborwa, serving Kruger National Park.

C

CAMPING and CARAVANNING

Good weather and good roads account for the popularity of camping and caravanning in South Africa. There are about 650 caravan (trailer) parks around the country, often in beautiful surroundings. Many have tent sites and amenities for campers too. Facilities at most sites are relatively lavish: hot and cold showers and bathrooms, laundries, rooms for ironing clothes and washing dishes and, in some cases, swimming pools, recreational halls, restaurants and shops. Popular parks, especially near the beaches, are likely to be full from mid-December to mid-January and at Easter.

You can rent a fully equipped caravan and the car to tow it, or, less widely available, a self-contained motor caravan (camper). Although hired cars can usually be picked up in one city and returned in another, caravans must go back to the point of hire if a collection charge is to be avoided.

CAR HIRE (RENTAL) (See also DRIVING on page 106, and PLANNING YOUR BUDGET on page 115)

Some well-known international and local car-hire firms have offices at airports, in all big cities and even small towns throughout South Africa. The local companies usually have slightly lower tariffs. Cars offered are normally South African–built Japanese or German models, from two-door compacts with manual gearshift to big four-door automatics with air-conditioning. You need a valid driver's licence and usually a minimum age (23 or 25) is specified. A cash deposit may be required unless a recognised credit card is used for payment. Rates include basic insurance and sometimes collision damage waiver and personal accident insurance as well. There may be a per-kilometre charge. Fuel is not included. Rates will usually be lower if you reserve a car before arriving in South Africa, perhaps as part of a package booked through a travel agent. Chauffeur-driven cars are also available. As a rule, hire cars may not cross South Africa's borders.

CHILDREN'S SOUTH AFRICA

The young will take to the pools and beaches with glee, but pay attention to warnings about currents, jellyfish, and other hazards. You're advised to restrict the time children spend in the sun, especially at first, and to apply plenty of high-protection sun-screen.

South Africa

CLIMATE

The seasons are reversed south of the equator: July is mid-winter and Christmas can be hot. Arriving from a Northern Hemisphere winter, you may find the customs men wearing shorts. Winter nights can be cold, especially at higher altitudes – and that includes Johannesburg – though daytime temperatures are often delightful. In the parks and reserves game-spotting is easiest in winter (from July to October). Because it's dry then, there's much less foliage to afford cover to the animals.

CLOTHING

Even in summer, a degree of formality is appropriate after dark. A sign in your hotel may say: 'Gentlemen are requested to wear long trousers to dinner. Beachwear is not acceptable at any time in the restaurant.' In the more exclusive hotels and restaurants jackets and ties are recommended, though perhaps not obligatory.

At holiday resorts and while you're in transit, very casual clothing suffices. Fancy safari suits are quite unnecessary in the game parks; anything comfortable will do, though darker colours seem to attract fewer insects.

For South African summers, pack lightweight clothing, and a light jacket or sweater for the occasional chilly evening. A raincoat or umbrella also would be useful; summer is the rainy season in much of the country, though generally it's a matter of a passing thunderstorm to relieve the heat. (An exception is the Mediterranean-style Western Cape, which is dry all summer with rain in the winter.) On the Natal coast the Indian Ocean is swimmable all the year round.

Temperatures	J	F	M	A	M	J	J	A	S	O	N	D
Cape Town												
Max °C	26	27	26	23	20	18	17	18	19	21	24	25
Max °F	79	80	79	74	68	64	63	64	66	70	75	77
Min °C	16	16	15	13	11	9	8	9	10	12	14	15
Min °F	61	61	59	55	52	48	46	48	50	54	57	59

Johannesburg

Max °C	26	26	24	22	19	16	16	20	23	25	25	26
Max °F	79	79	75	72	66	61	61	68	74	77	77	79
Min °C	14	13	13	10	7	4	4	6	9	12	13	14
Min °F	57	55	55	50	45	39	39	43	48	54	55	57

CRIME

As in much of the world, burglaries and muggings are becoming commonplace in South African cities. Be prepared to find steel security gates and guards at restaurants, shops, and car parks (parking lots). It makes sense to lock your property out of sight in the boot (trunk) of your car and always lock the doors. Use the hotel safe for any valuables. And don't go out flashing jewellery, walking alone at night, or otherwise inviting trouble.

CUSTOMS and ENTRY FORMALITIES

Passport holders from the USA, EU countries, Australia and New Zealand no longer require a visa to visit South Africa. However, as visa regulations are subject to change, it is wise to check with your travel agent or the nearest South African embassy or consulate. Alternatively, you can write to the Director General, Home Affairs:

Private Bag X114, Pretoria 0001, South Africa, tel: (021) 314-8911.

If you require a visa make sure you allow plenty of time for the application to be processed. If you plan to include a visit to any neighbouring countries and then return to South Africa, you should include this information on your application so that you receive a multiple-entry visa. Opening and closing times of border posts may be obtained by contacting the Department of Home Affairs, tel: (011) 314-8130, fax: (011) 326-6309.

On the plane, you'll be given a form to fill in. Present this on arrival to the Passport Control Officer, who will fix a temporary residence permit in your passport specifying the length and purpose of the stay. You may need to show a return ticket and some proof that you can support yourself in South Africa.

Here are the main items you may take into South Africa duty-free and, on your return home, into your own country:

Into:	Cigarettes		Cigars		Tobacco	Spirits		Wine
S. Africa	400	and	50	and	250g	1*l*	and	2*l*
Australia	200	or	250g	or	250g	1*l*	or	1*l*
Canada	200	and	50	and	900g	1.1*l*	or	1.1*l*
Ireland	200	or	50	or	250g	1*l*	and	2*l*
N. Zealand	200	or	50	or	250g	1.1*l*	and	4.5*l*
UK	200	or	50	or	250g	1*l*	and	2*l*
USA	200	and	100	and	*	1*l*	or	1*l**

*A reasonable quantity.

Currency restrictions. Visitors may take any amount of foreign currency (travellers' cheques are obviously safer than cash) into South Africa. Large amounts should be declared upon arrival. The South African currency you may carry in or out is limited to R500.

DRIVING

With 45,000km (27,900 miles) of paved road, much of it excellent, South Africa is well suited for touring by car. There are some stretches of toll road, but the charges are quite modest. Away from the cities traffic is light and you can keep up high average speeds. Even dirt roads to more remote destinations are usually well graded.

Paperwork. You must have a valid driving licence with the details printed in English, or an accompanying certificate of authenticity in English, or an international licence, obtained before arrival in South Africa. To hire a car, there are no unusual requirements (*see Car Hire*), but if you plan to import a car, advance planning and documentation are complicated. For details, consult SATOUR (*see*

Tourist Information Offices) or the Automobile Association of South Africa:

66 De Korte Street, Braamfontein, Johannesburg 2001
(tel: 011 407-1000 or 0-800-010-101 (toll-free); <www.aasa.co.za>

Driving conditions. As part of the British legacy, South Africa drives on the left. If you're not accustomed to it, start slowly and be especially vigilant when making turns. The speed limit on main highways is 120 km/h (75 mph). Elsewhere, the indicated limit may be 100 km/h or 80 km/h (50 mph) and you are generally restricted to 60 km/h (37 mph) in built-up areas unless otherwise posted. Driving standards are variable and the accident rate is high. In rural areas watch out for animals and pedestrians on the roads.

Police patrol cars are seen mostly near the cities and towns; if you break the law, you may be fined on the spot.

Road signs. Standard international pictographs are used for most situations, but there are some South African peculiarities. Printed signs are bilingual, eg, 'Border/Grens' or 'Ompad/Detour', or they alternate, so remember that Kaapstad means Cape Town and is not some new destination. (There is no town named 'Slegs'. The frequently seen 'Slegs Only' with an arrow merely means the lane in question must only be used for turning. 'Only'is 'slegs' in Afrikaans. 'Net' also means 'only'.)

Parking restrictions are indicated by letters in circles painted on the road surface. Parking meters in most cities take a variety of coins.'

'L' means loading zone (goods vehicles only); 'B' means reserved for buses, 'T' for taxis and 'FB' for fire-fighting equipment. 'S' with a diagonal stripe means no stopping, a striped 'P' is a no-parking indicator. Traffic lights are called 'robots', in English and Afrikaans.

Fuel. Filling stations are found on all main roads, although in country areas they're widely dispersed. Most stations are open only between 7am and 7pm, Monday to Saturday, but every town has one or more station open for longer hours. Grades of fuel available are 93 and 97 octane (but 87 and 93 in Johannesburg and the rest of the Witwatersrand because of the high altitude). Most stations offer full service and attendants are ready to clean the windscreen and check oil and water. Note: petrol (gasoline) cannot be purchased with credit cards.

Driving in the game parks and reserves. The Kruger National Park in particular is geared to the motor car, with about 900km (558 miles) of tarred roads, plus 1,500km (930 miles) of gravel roads. The speed limit is generally 50km/h (31mph), but slow driving gives animal pedestrians a better chance of survival, and you are more likely to sight game in the bush at 25km/h (15mph) than at 50km/h (30mph)– and on gravel or dirt roads you'll kick up much less dust.

Animals seem to consider the cars just another species of wild life, but out of your car – even if you stick your head or arms out the window – you become a recognisable human, frightening some animals and prompting others to attack. This is why you must stay in the car anywhere beyond the fenced camps, barring an emergency. Park authorities emphasise that there are no tame animals, not even the lovable-looking vervet monkeys, which may bite. Feeding any animal is strictly forbidden.

Some more regulations: you may not drive off an authorised road into the bush or on to a road with a 'no entry' sign. Among other dangers, if your car should break down in an unauthorised place, help might not reach you for days. Any firearms must be declared and sealed at the gate. No pets are allowed.

One rule that is taken very seriously in the parks is the closing of the gates. In winter you must be back in your camp, or out of the park, by 5.30pm; in summer by 6.30pm. If you're five minutes late you'll be subject to a fine. The excuse that the road was blocked by elephants has been invented so often that it is no longer accepted, even when true. Night travel is forbidden in the national parks to protect animals and also to make life more difficult for poachers.

For park bookings within South Africa, ring the National Parks Board in Pretoria; tel: (012) 343-1991.

Fluid measures

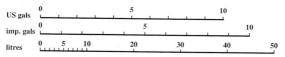

Distance

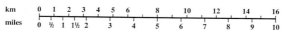

E

ELECTRICITY

Voltage is generally 220/230 volts AC, 50 cycles (but Pretoria's is 250V). South Africa uses plugs with three round pins. Hardware stores and supermarkets sell adapters for electric razors and other appliances.

EMBASSIES and CONSULATES

(See also the *Yellow Pages* of local telephone directories under 'Consulates and Embassies'.)

Australia:	Mutual and Federal Building, 292 Orient Street, Arcadia, Pretoria. Tel: (012) 342-3740 14th floor, BP Centre, Long Street, Cape Town. Tel: (021) 419-5425
Canada:	1103 Arcadia Street, Hatfield, Pretoria. Tel: (012) 324-6923
Ireland:	Delheim Suite, Tubach Centre, 1234 Church Street, Pretoria.

South Africa

	Tel: (012) 342-5062
UK:	255 Hill Street, Arcadia, Pretoria.
	Tel: (012) 483 1200
	1st Floor, Southern Life Centre, 8 Riebeeck Street, Cape Town.
	Tel: (021) 405-2400
	275 Jan Smuts Avenue, Dunkeld West, Johannesburg.
	Tel: (011) 537-7000
	19th floor, The Marine, 22 Gardiner Street, Durban.
	Tel: (031) 305-3041
U.S.A.:	Thibault House, 877 Pretorius Street, Pretoria.
	Tel: (012) 342-1048
	Broadway Industries Centre, Heerengracht, Cape Town.
	Tel: (021) 21 4280
	1 River Street, Killarney, Johannesburg.
	Tel: (011) 644-8000

EMERGENCIES

Police flying squad:	telephone 1-0111	
Ambulance:	telephone 999	
Fire Brigade:	Johannesburg	Tel: 999
	Cape Town	Tel: 535-1100
	Durban	Tel: 361-0000
Information (electronic *Yellow Pages*):	All towns/cities	Tel: 10118

ETIQUETTE

Because of the adverse publicity the country has received in most of the world, you'll find some sensitivity to the views of foreigners, so it's wise not to overstate any political opinions. If you want to take pictures of black tribal dances, first find out if there are any objections.

G

GETTING TO SOUTH AFRICA

It's possible to go by container ship, cargo boat, or even as part of a cruise, but most visitors fly. Although the fares and conditions described below have all been carefully checked, it is well worth consulting a travel agent for the latest information.

Scheduled flights. You can fly to South Africa from North America direct and via a number of European cities, including Athens, London, Frankfurt, Lisbon, Paris, Rome and Zurich.

There are non-stop flights from London Heathrow to Johannesburg, where a connecting service is offered to Cape Town, Durban, Port Elizabeth and other cities. Several airlines also operate direct services to Cape Town and Durban. You may also fly via one of South Africa's neighbours, perhaps making a stopover on the way.

The months of January, July and December are peak season for fares. April and May fares are lowest. Round the World (RTW) fares offered for certain routes include a stop in South Africa.

Charter flights and package tours

From North America: All-inclusive package tours are available. Costs covered include the round-trip airfare (usually from New York), accommodation, most or all meals, transfers, baggage handling, local transport and sightseeing.

From the UK: Tour operators offer a variety of holidays with everything included, as well as land-only packages if you wish to arrange your own air travel. Certain airlines can obtain hotel and car-hire (rental) discounts for their passengers. The South African Tourism Board, or SATOUR (see TOURIST INFORMATION OFFICES on page 122) gives information on tours and package holidays.

Some charter flights are currently offered to Johannesburg, but you must reserve far ahead as space fills up quickly.

South Africa

GUIDES and TOURS

City sightseeing tours and day excursions to beauty spots are normally led by bilingual (English and Afrikaans) guides. For interpreters of other languages, check with the local tourist office. Package tours of Kruger National Park are led by experienced guides who can help spot the animals and identify them. In the private game parks rangers are able to give attention to visitors' individual interests, such as bird-watching.

LANGUAGE

The official languages are English and Afrikaans, although black people speak one or more of 11 other principal languages, and Asians, six. Most of the whites and 'coloureds' (people of mixed race) claim Afrikaans (derived from Dutch) as their mother tongue. In practice, you'll find most people understand English, but here are a few phrases you might try in an Afrikaans environment. Note that the 'g' is pronounced as a throaty 'kh', and 'oe' is pronounced 'oo'.

Good morning	**Goeie môre**
Good afternoon	**Goeie middag**
Good night	**Goeie nag**
Please	**Asseblief**
Thank you	**Dankie**
Goodbye	**Tot siens**

Many common Afrikaans words and expressions have been borrowed by English-speakers in South Africa. Here are some distinctive words that you are likely to hear:

bakkie	pickup truck
braai	barbecue
combi	microbus or minibus

dorp	small town
kop/koppie	hilltop/small hill
rondavel	circular hut/house
robot	traffic light
tackies	sports shoes
tickey-box	pay phone
tsotsi	mugger, street criminal

M

MAPS

SATOUR *(see page 123)* issues (free) excellent tourist maps of South Africa and the regions. Local information offices, car-hire firms and the Automobile Association (for AA members) are also sources of free maps. Extremely detailed, indexed maps of cities and regions are sold at bookstores.

MEDICAL MATTERS

Vaccinations. No vaccinations are required for entry into South Africa unless you are arriving from a yellow-fever zone, when you must have an international yellow-fever vaccination certificate.

Malaria preventative tablets should be taken by everyone planning to visit the Transvaal Lowveld (Kruger Park or the private game parks nearby), Zululand in Natal, or certain areas of South Africa's neighbours. Ask your pharmacist or doctor to explain the precautions you must take. Or you can go to any pharmacy in South Africa and buy anti-malaria pills over the counter. Normally, you must start taking the pills several days before entering the affected district and continue the specified dosage for several weeks after leaving. A syrup is available for children.

As an additional precaution, try to avoid being bitten by mosquitoes, one variety of which is responsible for spreading the disease. Apply an insect repellent, cover up your skin outdoors after dusk, and keep mosquitoes out of your sleeping area, by using mosquito netting and/or air-conditioning.

Other problems. Apart from 'bluebottles' (men-of-war jellyfish) and tides, swimming in the ocean presents no special problems. However, be extremely careful about rivers and lakes: unless otherwise announced, they may be inhabited by the dangerous bilharzia parasite, which can be contracted by ingesting unpurified water or through bare feet or skin in or near the water. Never drink from a river unless you've been assured its water is potable.

Most of the 140 varieties of snake in South Africa are harmless, or almost, but if the worst happens, anti-snakebite serum is available.

Beware of the power of the sun. You can feel cool by the sea, or at higher altitudes, and still burn. Doctors recommend strict limits on exposure and using a sunscreen with a protection factor of at least 15.

Insurance. Since South Africa has no national health service, any medical treatment and hospitalization must be paid for direct. If you have medical insurance already, make certain that it covers foreign countries. Otherwise, take out special travel insurance that includes coverage of accidents, illness, or hospitalisation on your trip.

Doctors. Most hotels have a list of nearby doctors in case of need. Or look in the white pages of the telephone directory under 'Mediese Praktisyns' or 'Medical Practitioners'.

Hospitals. All cities have well-equipped hospital facilities, some of international repute.

Pharmacies. In the big cities one pharmacy (chemist) in each area stays open after normal business hours. Check in the local newspaper for details of late opening hours.

MONEY MATTERS

Currency. The unit of currency of South Africa is the rand (R), divided into 100 cents (c). South Africa is currently in the process of changing its coins and notes, so for a while there will be a dual system of old and new coins and notes in circulation.

Coins: 1, 2, 5 (being phased out), 10, 20, and 50c; R1 and R2 (a small coin, easily mistaken for one of lesser value).

Banknotes: R5 (being phased out), R10, R20, R50, R100, and R200. The R200 note looks a lot like the R20, so be alert.

For currency restrictions, see CUSTOMS AND ENTRY FORMALITIES.

Banking hours. Monday to Friday 9am–3.30pm, Saturday 8.30am–11am (later in major cities). Small-town banks may close for lunch from 12.45pm–2pm (except Wednesday and Saturday).

Credit cards and travellers' cheques. All commercial banks cash travellers' cheques in any major hard currency. Many hotels and shops also welcome travellers' cheques. Major international credit cards are accepted in most hotels, many shops and by tour operators and carriers. Some bank branches will advance cash against a major credit card. Automated Teller Machines (ATMs) are available in major cities and towns for those on the Cirrus and Plus systems.

Taxes. VAT at a standard rate (currently 14 percent) is charged on all purchases of goods and services, except on some basic foodstuffs. It is included in the prices advertised. VAT. may be reclaimed when the total value of items taken out of the country exceeds R250. For information on the refund process, contact the VAT. Refund Administrators, P.O. Box 107, Johannesburg International Airport Post Office, 1627, tel: (011) 390-2970.

Planning your Budget

The following are some prices in South African rands (R). However, they must be taken as an approximate guide; inflation is a factor in South Africa as elsewhere.

Airport transfers. SAA bus from Johannesburg International Airport to central Johannesburg: R35.00, to Pretoria: R60.00; taxi to central

South Africa

Johannesburg R150 upwards; taxi from Cape town International Airport to central Cape Town: R75–90.

Car hire (international company). *VW Golf:* about R200 per day for up to 14 days. *Minibus:* about R600 per day. Prices include collision damage waiver, other insurance and VAT.

Cigarettes. R7.50. (Imported brands cost more.)

Excursions. Full-day Cape Peninsula tour from Cape Town: R375–400; three-day Johannesburg–Kruger Park coach tour including most meals, entry fees and accommodation (shared room, per person): R3,050; three-day Johannesburg–Sun City coach tour including most meals and accommodation in double room: R2,400 per person.

Hairdressers. *Man's* haircut: R30–R50 (tip expected); *Woman's* haircut, shampoo, set and blow-dry: R80–150 (tip expected).

Hotels (double room with bath). ***** R1,500–3,500, *** R600+ with breakfast, * R200+ with breakfast.

Meals and drinks. (medium-priced restaurant). Lunch: R50–70; dinner: R80–120; bottle of wine: R70 upwards; beer: R7 upward; liquor R8 upward; soft drink: R5 upward.

National Parks. Entry fees: R10–30 per person; R24 per car. Lodges: R130 per person (approximately).

Petrol (gasoline). R3.75–R4.20 per litre.

Taxis. Fares vary from town to town. For safety, stick to metered taxis and avoid informal. mini-bus style cabs. Meters start at about R5, plus R2.50 per km (tip expected).

Trains (one way). Johannesburg–Cape Town, normal train: R450–650; Blue Train, standard compartment (per person, meals included): R18,300 upwards. Johannesburg–Pretoria: R30; Johannesburg–Durban: R200–300.

O

OPENING HOURS

Business hours are typically from 8.30am to 4.30pm. Most shops stay open from 8.30am to 5pm Monday to Friday and until 12.30pm on Saturday. Some greengrocers, pharmacies, bookshops and super-markets may stay open later. Cafés (essentially small general stores) may operate from 6am to midnight seven days a week. Some big shopping centres stay open till 5pm on Saturday and from 9am to 1pm on Sunday. Beachfront shops of all kinds in Durban stay open all day on Sunday.

Cango Caves, Oudtshoorn: December, January, February and April, tours for visitors every hour from 8am to 5pm, off-season every second hour from 9am to 3pm.

Gold Reef City, Johannesburg: rides and displays: 9.30am to 5pm, Tuesday to Sunday; entertainment and bars: to 11pm, Tuesday to Saturday and to 7pm on Sunday.

Kruger National Park opens from 5am to 6.30pm in summer and from 6.30am to 5.30pm in winter.

Premier Diamond Mine, Cullinan, near Pretoria: tours at 9am and 10.30am Monday to Friday (not for children under 10). Tours take an hour and a half.

State Opera and Theatre complex, Pretoria: guided tours take place at 11am on Monday, Wednesday and Friday and at 4.30pm on Wednesday.

Stock Exchange, Johannesburg: guided tours at 11am and 2.30pm Monday to Friday.

Voortrekker Monument, Pretoria: 9am to 4pm, Monday and Wednesday to Saturday, and 11am to 4pm on Sunday, but closed on Good Friday and Christmas Day.

P

PHOTOGRAPHY and VIDEOS

Some, but not all, international brands of film are on sale. Same-day colour printing is available in most cities and larger resorts. Keep your film as cool as possible in the semi-tropical regions. Never leave your camera locked in a car parked in the hot sun.

It's worth carrying spare batteries, and if you've just bought a new camera, taking some test pictures before you leave home. Check that your travel insurance covers your equipment.

Photographing wild life requires fast film – at least ASA 200 – because the subject may move, and so may your long lens. Even if you don't have a telephoto or zoom lens, many animals come so close that you can still get some good pictures.

Airport security machines use X-rays, which are safe for normal film, exposed or not. If you have extra-fast film, ask that it be checked separately. Videotape is available for all standard video cameras. They can be hired at some attractions.

POLICE

Members of the national police force, who are armed, wear blue uniforms and peaked caps. In the cities they usually drive small 'Black Maria' vans (actually yellow) with caged space for culprits. The traffic police wear khaki.

POST OFFICES

Most post offices are open from 8.30am to 4.30pm Monday to Friday and 8am to noon on Saturday. Smaller offices close for lunch from 1pm to 2pm.

They deal with a complicated variety of services, from issuing television licences to dealing with pensions, so you may have to wait for your postage stamps. Mail boxes, many of them bearing the monograms of British sovereigns, are painted red. Service is reasonably fast for overseas mail.

Poste restante. If you're not sure where you'll be staying, you may have mail addressed to you *poste restante* (general delivery). The main post offices – on Parliament Street in Cape Town, West Street in Durban – and Jeppe Street in Johannesburg, Church Square in Pretoria, have special counters for this service.

Telegrams. The post office handles electronic communications as well. Any branch office will accept your telegram. The main post offices in Johannesburg and Cape Town have a cable and telegraph counter available 24 hours a day.

PUBLIC HOLIDAYS

January 1	New Year's Day
March 21	Human Rights' Day
April 27	Freedom Day
May 1	Workers' Day
June 16	Youth Day
August 9	National Women's Day
September 24	Heritage Day
December 16	Day of Reconciliation
December 25/26	Xmas Day/Goodwill Day

Movable dates:
Good Friday, Family Day (Easter Monday).

PUBLIC TRANSPORT

Buses. In Johannesburg the Publicity Association sells reduced-rate tickets for unlimited travel on the buses except at peak hours. Bus-route maps and timetables are also sold at the City Hall, Market Street. Evening services are sparse, and from 2pm on Saturday until Monday morning all municipal buses depart from the station at Main and Rissik streets.

Bus services in other cities are less complex – local information offices will help. In all buses, even the double-deckers, you pay the driver on the way in. Keep your ticket, as an inspector is likely to board the bus to double-check.

Trains. Many South African trains are fascinating. Hundreds of steam locomotives still earn their keep – a thrill for train buffs. Several narrow-gauge lines still operate, including the Apple Express west from Port Elizabeth to Avontuur – 285km (177 miles) of 61-cm (2-ft) gauge railway. At the other end of the scale the Blue Train *(see page 83)*, the pride of South African Railways, maintains five-star luxury between Pretoria and Cape Town. All long-distance trains have sleeping compartments in first and second class. Daily commuter trains are far less glamorous.

R

RADIO and TELEVISION

There has been a veritable explosion of new radio stations following a new system brought in to replace the apartheid-era monopoly of radio by the South African Broadcasting Corporation (SABC). There are now some 65 community stations representing a wide spectrum of interests, from universities to religious and ethnic groupings. Meanwhile, the SABC transmits various services on FM, including the English Service – a mix of news, music and features; the Afrikaans Service; and Radio 5, which specialises in pop music. In addition, there are regional services (strong on pop) on AM and FM, and stations broadcasting in the major black languages. BBC, Voice of America and European shortwave stations can be picked up; BBC and VOA also use a medium-wave frequency for southern Africa.

The English/Afrikaans television channel, TV1, divides the day equally between the two languages. The CCV (Contemporary Community Values) channel and NNTV broadcast in English and African languages. M-Net is an independent subscription station showing films, sports, and entertainment. Various satellite TV channels also broadcast.

T

TAXIS

In South African cities the taxis do not normally cruise for fares. You must go to a taxi rank or ask your hotel desk clerk to call a cab by phone. In Johannesburg taxis are usually found outside the Carlton Centre in Kruis Street. In Cape Town a likely taxi rank is opposite the Air Terminal in Lower Adderley Street. The word taxi also applies to the many minibuses which ply fixed routes.

TELEPHONES

South Africa's automatic network functions efficiently, and you can dial direct to many other countries. The international access code is 09. (The country code to use in IDD calls to South Africa is 27.)

Calls within South Africa are cheaper between 6pm and 8pm from Monday to Friday and cheapest between 8pm and 7am, and from 1pm on Saturday to 7am on Monday.

Coin-operated telephones in street boxes, cafés, and public places take 20c, 50c, and R1 coins. Directions are given in English and Afrikaans. Phone cards in R10 denominations are available at post offices and other outlets. They can be used at green public telephones for calls within South Africa and international calls. In Johannesburg an international telephone office on the ground floor of the Post Office building in Smal Street is open 24 hours a day. Cellphones (mobiles) are extremely popular and can be hired at Johannesburg International Airport. For local directory assistance: 1023; national directory assistance: 1025.

TIME DIFFERENCES

All year round, South Africa stays on GMT + 2. For example, during (northern) winter:

Los Angeles	New York	London	**South Africa**	Sydney
2am	5am	10am	**noon**	9pm

South Africa

TIPPING

In South Africa tipping is less generous than in most of Europe and North America. Tips are expected, but not always received, by filling station attendants, hotel maids, railway porters, taxi drivers, waiters, stewards and caddies.

Some suggestions:

Hairdresser	10 percent
Maid, per week	R20–25
Porter, per bag	R5
Taxi driver	10 percent
Tour guide	10 percent
Waiter	10 percent if service charge is not included

TOURIST INFORMATION OFFICES

About 50 South African cities and towns have Publicity Associations or similar organisations for the benefit of visitors. They issue pamphlets and maps, give advice, and often help with hotel reservations. Some of the big ones:

Johannesburg: Publicity Association, Ground Floor, North State Building, corner Market and Kruis streets, P.O. Box 4580, Johannesburg 2000. 24-hour tourist information service, tel: (011) 331-9330; fax (011) 331-9351

Pretoria: Information Bureau, Munitoria Building, corner Vermeulen and Van der Walt Streets. Tel: (012) 313-8259; fax: (012) 313-8460

Durban: Publicity Association and Visitors' Bureau, West Street, corner of Church Street. Tel: (031) 304-4934; fax: (031) 304-6196

Cape Town: Tourism Authority (Captour), The Pinnacle, corner Burg and Castle streets, Cape Town. Tel: (021) 426-4260

Each main centre also has a South African Tourism Board (SATOUR) office that is able to provide countrywide information, including brochures, maps and accommodation details. The main office in Johannesburg is very helpful and able to answer most enquires. Addresses and telephone and fax numbers are given on all major SATOUR publications. The head office postal address is:

Private Bag: X10012, Sandton 2146
Tel: (011) 778-8000; fax (011) 778-8001

SATOUR offices abroad:

UK 5–6 Alt Grove, Wimbledon, London SW19 4DZ. Tel: (020) 8971 9350 fax: (020) 8944 6705

USA 500 Fifth Avenue, 20th Floor, New York, NY 10110. Tel: (212) 730-2929 or (800) 822-5368; fax: (212) 760-1980
Suite 1524, 9841 Airport Boulevard, Los Angeles, CA90045. Tel: (310) 641-8444 or (800) 782-9772; fax (310) 641-5812

Australia SAA offices, Level 6, 285 Clarence Street, Sydney 2000.Tel: (02) 4261-3424

Zimbabwe Office 106, Sanlam Centre, Newlands, Harare. Tel: (4) 7464876; fax: (4) 746489

TRAVELLERS WITH DISABILITIES

Great advances have been made in recent years in the provision of special toilet facilities and wheelchair access to public buildings, hotels, and other places visitors might want to go. The SATOUR book, Where to Stay (see ACCOMMODATION), gives details of such facilities, and the Independence Living Center, <www.independentliving.org> can also advise on specific facilities and services.

WATER

You can drink tap water anywhere in South Africa – even in the game parks. In some coastal areas it may be tinted by iron deposits, but it's still potable.

WEIGHTS AND MEASURES

Length

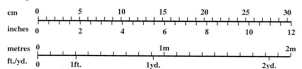

Weight

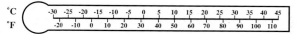

Temperature

YOUTH HOSTELS

For full information, check out the website of Hostelling International South Africa (HISA), <www.hisa.org.za>, or contact them at St George's House, 3rd floor, 73 St George's Mall, Cape Town 8001; Tel: (021) 424-2511; fax: (021) 424-4119. They can supply a list of Youth Hostels around the country. YMCA and YWCA hostels can be found in the cities, but they are more expensive than the youth hostels.

Recommended Hotels

In the following pages we offer a short selection of establishments in the areas covered in the WHERE TO GO section of this book (and in the same order). The list is by no means exhaustive, but is designed to give you a few pointers by selecting places which offer something extra in the way of facilities, location, character, or value for money. We have included some of the private game lodges, but camps in the national parks (see page 42) are not listed here for reasons of space.

Our ratings are an indication of the cost per person, sharing a double room, with breakfast. Many country retreats and game lodges only publish rates for dinner, bed, and breakfast, however. Note that there may be very wide seasonal variations, and these prices are only approximate as the rapid inflation of recent years seems likely to continue. Also, depending on their rating, SATOUR-graded hotels add a surcharge from R1.70 to R5.70.

$	R200+
$$	R250+
$$$	R600+
$$$$	R1,500–R3,000

JOHANNESBURG AREA

Capri $$$ *27 Aintree Avenue, Savoy Estates, Bramley 2018; Tel: (011) 786-2250; Fax: (011) 887-2286.* 50 rooms. Attractive northern garden suburb location. Pool, tennis.

The Westcliff $$$$ *67 Jan Smuts Avenue, Westcliff 2193; Tel: (011) 6446 2400; Fax: (011) 6446 2401.* 115 rooms. Luxurious modern hotel perched on a ridge and enjoying spectacular views over the city. Pool, health club.

South Africa

Town Lodge $$$ *Herman Road, Harmelia Ext 2, Germiston; Tel: (011) 974 5202; Fax: (011) 974 7126. 135 rooms.* Just 5km (3 miles) from Johannesburg International Airport, this hotel offers a handy airport shuttle bus service to ensure you catch your flight. Air-conditioned rooms with TV and shower.

Holiday Inn Garden Court $$$$ *Corner West and Maude streets, Sandton 2146; Tel: (011) 734-1366; Fax: (011) 734 8202.* 444 rooms in the city's premier residential and business district. Pool deck and garden.

Gold Reef City Hotel $$$$ *Golf Reef City, Johannesburg 2159; Tel: (011) 496-1626; Fax: (011) 496-1626, ext. 297.* 45 rooms. Built in 1890s style but with modern luxuries. Set in the Gold Reef City theme park.

Mercure Inn Randburg Waterfront $$ *Corner Republic and Randburg streets, Randburg Waterfront, Johannesburg 2438; Tel: (011) 762-4308; Fax: (011) 762-4491.* 104 rooms. Comfortable budget hotel close to excellent shopping and entertainment facilities.

Intercontinental Sandton Sun and Towers Johannesbsurg $$$$ *Fifth Street, Sandton City, P.O. Box 784902, Sandton 2146; Tel: (011) 780-5000; Fax: (011) 780-5002.* 334 rooms. Opulent modern tower adjoining a vast shopping complex. Glittering interior, pool, gardens, health club.

Sunnyside Park $$$ *2 York Road, Parktown, Johannesburg 2193; Tel: (011) 643-7226; Fax: (011) 642-0019.* 96 rooms. Gracious former residence of the British High Commissioner, situated in a park and garden setting. Pool.

PRETORIA

Arcadia $$ *515 Proes Street, Pretoria 0083; Tel: (012) 326-9311; Fax: (012) 326-1067.* 143 rooms in a centrally located modern block which is attached to a shopping mall.

Boulevard $$$ *186 Struben Street, Pretoria 0002; Tel: (012) 326-4806; Fax: (012) 326-1366.* 100 rooms. A modern business and conference hotel, conveniently located for business and government offices. Entertainment.

Crowne Plaza Holiday Inn $$$$ *Church Street/Beatrix Street, P.O. Box 40694, Pretoria 0007; Tel: (012) 341-1571; Fax: (012) 44-7534.* 241 rooms. Centrally located for government offices and cultural attractions. Pool, entertainment.

Protea Hof $$$ *Pretorius/Van der Walt streets, Pretoria 0002; Tel: (012) 322-7570; Fax: (012) 322-9461.* 116 rooms. Modern city-centre hotel; business facilities and entertainment.

SUN CITY

Cascades $$$$ *PO Box 7, Sun City 0316, Bophuthatswana; Information: Tel: (014) 557-1000; Reservations: (011) 780 7800.* 242 rooms. Complete resort, with casino, health centre, entertainment, pools, sports, including golf, tennis, squash, bowls. Sailing and windsurfing are both available at nearby Waterworld.

Kwa Maritane Bush Lodge $$$ *Pilanesburg National Park, Sun City 0316; Tel: (01465) 21820; Fax: (01465) 21621.* Hotel and resort in Pilanesburg National Park. Pool, tennis.

The Palace of the Lost City $$$$ *PO Box 308, Sun City 0316; Information: Tel: (014) 557-1000; Reservations: (011) 780 7800.* 338 rooms. Vast, exotic resort, with entertainment, casino, health centre, pools, sports, including golf, tennis, squash, bowls.

Sun City Hotel $$$$ *PO Box 2, Sun City 0316; Information: Tel: (014) 557-1000; Reservations: (011) 780 7800.* 340 rooms. Luxurious resort. Entertainment, casino, health centre, pools, sports, including golf, tennis, squash, bowls. Sailing and windsurfing available at nearby Waterworld.

MPUMALANGA AND LIMPOPO PROVINCES

Casa do Sol $$$ *P.O.Box 57, Hazyview; Tel/fax: (01317) 68111.* 40 rooms. Village of villas and cottages in woodlands. Pools, tennis, riding, fishing, game reserve.

The Chestnut Country Lodge $$$ *Ukuzwana Farm, Kiepersol, Hazyview 1242; Tel: (01317) 68780; Fax: (01317) 68783.* Farmstead, suites and cottages in lush gardens and farmland. Pool, bird-watching. Close to Numbi Gate of Kruger Park.

Hazyview Protea $$$$ *Burgershall, Hazyview 1242; Tel: (01317) 67332; Fax: (01317) 67335.* 48 rooms. Short drive from the Kruger Park and several private reserves. Set in large gardens with fine views. Pool, tennis.

Hulala Lakeside Lodge $$$ *P.O. Box 1382, White River 1240; Tel: (01311) 51710: Fax: same, ask for fax.* 21 rooms. Country-house hotel by lake. Pool. Bird-watching, fishing, windsurfing, canoeing on the lake.

Karos Lodge $$$ *P.O. Box 54, Skukuza 1350; Tel: (01311) 65671; Fax: (01311) 65676.* 96 rooms. Near the Kruger Gate of Kruger Park and various private reserves. Modern hotel in a bush setting. Pool, tennis.

Londolozi Game Reserve $$$$ *Sabi Sands, P.O. Box 6, Skukuza 1350; Tel: (reservations) (011) 809-4300; Fax: (reservations) (011) 809-4400.* 20 rooms. Luxury rondavels and bungalows. Pools, drives/walks in bush escorted by rangers, range of wildlife in surroundings.

Mala Mala Game Reserve $$$$ *Sabi Sand, via Skukuza 1353; Tel: (031) 765-2900; Fax: (031) 765-3365.* 50 rooms. One of the most luxurious of the game lodges, with chalets in an idyllic setting. Pools. Experienced game rangers on staff.

Motswari Game Lodge $$$$ *Timbavati Game Reserve; Tel: (011) 463-1990; Fax: (011) 463-1992.* 23 rooms. Luxury rondavels, pool. The game reserve is adjacent to Kruger Park.

Mount Sheba Country Lodge $$$ *Above Pilgrim's Rest, P.O. Box 100, Pilgrim's Rest 1290; Tel: (01315) 81241; Fax: (01315) 81248.* 25 rooms in own nature reserve. Hilltop and forest setting, thatched stone houses. Pool, walks, bird-watching.

Ngala Game Lodge $$$$ *Timbavati Game Reserve; Tel: (011) 803-8421; Fax: (reservations) (011) 803-1810.* 22 rooms in luxury thatched chalets, pool. Rangers escort walks and drives through the bush.

Numbi $$$ *P.O. Box 6, Hazyview 1242; Tel/fax: (01317) 377301.* 22 rooms. Close to Kruger Park. Main hotel and garden chalets, well equipped. Pool, tennis.

Sabi Sabi Game Reserve $$$$ *Sabi Sand, Skukuza 1350; Tel: (011) 483-3939; Fax: (011) 483-3799.* 45 rooms. Luxury lodges amid big-game area bordering Kruger Park. Pools. Rangers take you on day and night safaris.

Singita Boulder Lodge $$$$ *Sabi Sand Game Reserve; Tel: (011) 784-7077; Fax: (011) 784-7667.* Six luxury suites, each with pool.

Thornybush $$$$ *Timbavati, via Hoedspruit; Tel: (015283) 1976; Fax: (011) 883-8201.* 31 rooms. Beautifully appointed thatched chalets and pool overlook bush near Kruger Park. Day and night walks escorted by rangers and trackers. Wide range of game.

South Africa

KWAZULU-NATAL INLAND
Cathedral Peak Hotel $$$ *Near Winterton, KwaZulu-Natal 3340; Tel: (036) 488-1888; Fax: (036) 488-1889.* 90 rooms. Resort and a fine base for walking and exploring in the Drakensberg. Thatched cottages and suites, pool, tennis, bowls, squash, riding, and fishing.

Champagne Sports Resort $$$ *Private Bag X9, Winterton 3340; Tel: (036) 468-1088; Fax: (036) 468-1072.* 50 rooms. Hotel and thatched cottages in mountain scenery. Tennis, bowls, squash, riding, golf, pool.

Granny Mouse's Country House $$$ *P.O. Box 22, Balgowan, KwaZulu-Natal 3275; Tel: (03324) 4071; Fax: (03324) 4229.* 19 rooms. Thatched-house complex in woodland setting. Pool, fishing, bird-watching, walks.

Karos Mont aux Sources $$$ *Private Bag X1670, Mont aux Sources 3353; Tel/fax: (036) 438-6230.* 72 rooms. Close to Royal Natal National Park. Mountain resort of luxury lodges, pool, sports, including tennis, squash, fishing, bowls.

Rob Roy $$ *P.O. Box 10, Botha's Hill, KwaZulu-Natal 3660; Tel: (031) 777-1305; Fax: (031) 777-1364.* 37 rooms. Resort hotel overlooking the Valley of a Thousand Hills, between Durban and Pietermaritzburg. Pool, tennis, squash.

Royal Hotel $$ *Murchison Street, Ladysmith 3370; Tel/fax: (0361) 22176.* 60 rooms. Mementoes of the famous siege. Pool, garden, base for visits to the Drakensberg.

Sandford Park Lodge $$$ *P.O. Box 7, Bergville,KwaZulu-Natal 3350; Tel: (036) 448-1001; Fax: (036) 448-1047.* 26 rooms. Resort in garden and woodland setting in Drakensberg foothills. Pool, riding, bowls, fishing, bird-watching.

KWAZULU-NATAL COAST AND DURBAN

Blue Marlin $$ *P.O. Box 24, Scottburgh 4180; Tel: (039) 978-3361; Fax: (039) 976-0971.* 84 rooms. Resort on south coast.

Holiday Inn Durban Elangeni $$$$ *63 Snell Parade, Durban 4000; Tel: (031) 37-1321; Fax: (031) 32-5527.* 446 rooms. Towering, luxury hotel with ocean views and very close to the beach. Pools.

The Karos Edward $$$ *P.O. Box 105 Marine Parade, Durban 4000; Tel: (031) 37-3681; Fax: (031) 32-1692.* 90 rooms. Classic white block on the Golden Mile seafront.

Oyster Box Hotel $$$$ *2 Lighthouse Road, Umhlanga Rocks, Natal 4320; Tel: (031) 561-2233; Fax: (031) 561-4072.* 88 rooms. On the beach, amid tropical gardens, with pool, tennis and fishing.

Phinda Private Game Reserve $$$$ *near Mkuze, Natal; Tel: (011) 809-4300; Fax: (011) 809-4400.* 23 rooms. Luxury game lodge, involved in conservation and re-stocking programmes. Chalets in river and forest setting.

The Royal Hotel $$$$ *267 Smith Street, Durban 4000; Tel: (031) 333-6000; Fax: (031) 333-6002.* 272 rooms. Large, old, established and fully modernized luxury hotel in city centre. Nominated South Africa's best hotel for 5 consecutive years. Pool, squash, health club. Many restaurants.

EASTERN CAPE AND GARDEN ROUTE

Protea Edward Hotel $$$ *Belmont Terrace, Central; Port Elizabeth 6001; Tel/fax: (041) 56-2056.* 110 rooms. Centrally located in historic district, overlooking the bay.

Eight Bells Mountain Inn $$ *Route R328, P.O. Box 436, Mossel Bay 6500; Tel: (044) 631-0000; Fax: (044) 631-0004.* 24

rooms. Country estate in mountain scenery. Rondavels and log cabins. Pool, tennis, bowls, riding.

Elizabeth Sun $$$$ *La Roche Drive, Humewood 6013, Port Elizabeth; Tel: (041) 721859; Fax: (041) 721033.* 210 rooms. Luxury hotel on King's Beach. Pool, watersports.

Fancourt Hotel & Country Club $$$$ *Montagu Street, Blanco, near George, P.O. Box 2266, George 6530; Tel: (0441) 70-8282; Fax: (0441) 708352.* 126 rooms. Elegant country house and resort around golf course. Pools, beach club, walks.

Holiday Inn Garden Court $$$ *Baron van Rheede Street, P.O. Box 52, Oudtshoorn 6620; Tel: (04431) 2201; Fax: (04431) 3003.* 120 rooms. Convenient for Cango Caves as well as Oudtshoorn's ostrich farms. Pool, tennis.

Ocean View Hotel $$ *94 Bland Street, Mossel Bay 6500; Tel: (0444) 3711; Fax: (0444) 3711 ext 259.* 39 rooms. Small hotel with holiday flats in the town centre.

The Plettenberg $$$$ *40 Church Street, P.O. Box 719; Plettenberg Bay 6600; Tel: (04457) 32030; Fax: (04457) 32074.* 26 rooms. Luxurious Relais et Chateaux resort overlooking the sea. Pool.

Santos Protea $$$ *Santos Road, Mossel Bay 6500; Tel: (0444) 7103; Fax: (0444) 91-1945.* 58 rooms. Well-equipped beach hotel overlooking bay. Pool.

Tsitsikamma Lodge $$$ *N2 National Road, Storms River 6308; Tel: (042) 280-3802; Fax: (042) 280-3803.* 41 rooms. Hunting lodge. Base for Tsitsikamma National Parks.

CAPE TOWN AND CAPE PENINSULA

Alphen $$$ *Alphen Drive, P.O. Box 35, Constantia, Cape Town 7848; Tel: (021) 794-5011; Fax: (021) 794-5710.* 29

rooms. Magnificent historic estate in beautiful setting. Pool, sports centre with tennis, squash.

The Cellars-Hohenhort $$$ *Hohenhort Avenue, P.O. Box 270, Constantia, Cape Town 7848; Tel: (021) 794-2137; Fax: (021) 794-2149.* 53 rooms. New buildings amid gardens and woods recall the Cape Dutch tradition. Pool, walks.

Majoros Bed and Breakfast $$ *69 Helena Crescent, Graceland, Khayelitsha, Cape Town; Tel: (021) 361 3412.* Traditional African experience, complete with trip to a local 'shebeen' (pub) for a beer and to catch up on township gossip.

Greenways $$ *1, Torquay Avenue, Upper Claremont, Cape Town; Tel: (021) 761-1792; Fax: (021) 761-0878.* 14 rooms. Country mansion in spacious gardens, pool, croquet.

Lord Nelson Inn $$ *58 St George's Street, False Bay, Simonstown 7795; Tel: (021) 786-1386; Fax: (021) 786-1009.* Just 10 rooms.

Mount Nelson $$$$ *76 Orange Street, Gardens, Cape Town 8001; Tel: (021) 23-1000; Fax: (021) 24-7472.* 159 rooms. Celebrated luxury hotel in spacious gardens. Pool, tennis, squash, etc.

The Peninsula $$$$ *313 Beach Road, Sea Point, Cape Town 8061; Tel: (021) 439-8888; Fax: (021) 439-8886.* 40 rooms. Balconies overlooking seafront and beaches. Pool.

The Townhouse Hotel $$ *60 Corporation Street, Cape Town 8001; Tel: (021) 45-7050; Fax: (021) 45-3891.* 104 rooms. Quiet, central, business hotel. Pool, health club.

Victoria & Alfred Hotel $$$ *The Pierhead, The Waterfront, P.O. Box 50050; Vlaeberg, Cape Town 8002; Tel: (021) 419-6677; Fax: (021) 419-8955.* 68 rooms. Elegant hotel in dockside redevelopment area.

The Vineyard Hotel $ *Protea Road, P.O. Box 151, Newlands,Cape Town 7725; Tel: (021) 683-3044; Fax: (021) 683-3365.* 124 rooms. Historic country-house hotel that has been beautifully restored.

CAPE WINELANDS

The D'Ouwe Werf $ *30 Church Street, Stellenbosch 7600; Tel: (021) 887-4608; Fax: (021) 887-4626.* 25 rooms. Fine, elegantly restored old country inn, in the heart of this historic town. Pool, gardens.

Grande Roche $$$$ *Plantasie Street, P.O. Box 6038, Paarl 7620; Tel: (021) 863-2727; Fax: (021) 863-2220.* 29 rooms. Former historic Cape Dutch farm buildings converted into luxury suites. Pools, tennis, gym, outdoor theatre.

Cathbert Country Inn $$$ *On the R44 between Paarl and Franschhoek, Western Cape; Tel: (021) 874 1366.* In the foothills of the Simonsberg mountains, just 40 minutes from Cape Town. Suites with verandahs and secluded garden.

NORTH AND NORTHWESTERN CAPE PROVINCE

Holiday Inn Garden Court Kimberley $$$$ *Du Toitspan Road, P.O. Box 635, Kimberley 8300; Tel: (0531) 31751; Fax: (0531) 21814.* 120 rooms. Luxurious resort and business hotel. Pool, gardens, tennis, squash.

Waterwiel Protea $$$ *Voortrekker Street, Kakamas 8870; Tel: (054) 431-0838; Fax: (054) 431-0836.* 25 rooms. Small resort in the vicinity of the Augrabies Falls National Park. Pool, tennis.

Recommended Restaurants

Here we can give only a small selection from the wide range of different eating places found in the major cities and suburbs. We don't cover the small towns and country areas, where it is usual to eat at wherever you are staying: the hotels and game lodges have their own, often very good, restaurants. (See the preceding pages, "Recommended Hotels.")

When you telephone for a reservation, you can ask if the restaurant is licensed to sell wine, and if not, whether you may bring your own.

As a rough guide to prices, we have marked each entry with one, two or three $ symbols. These correspond to the approximate cost of a three-course dinner per person, not including drinks, as follows:

$	up to R100
$$	R100–200
$$$	over R200

JOHANNESBURG AREA

Anton Van Wouw $$ *111 Sivewright Avenue, Doornfontein; Tel: (011) 402-7916.* The former house of sculptor Anton van Wouw, with traditional South African meat and fish dishes available.

Cento $$ *100 Langerman Drive, Kensington; Tel: (011) 622-7272.* Mediterranean cuisine: Italian, seafood specialities. Extensive and impressive wine list. Reservations recommended.

El Em House of Prawns $$ *Corner Chaplin and Oxford roads, Illovo; Tel: (011) 447-2977.* Not only prawns any style, but plenty of other seafood and meat alternatives too.

Osteria Tre Nonni $$ *9 Grafton Avenue, Craighall Park; Tel: (011) 327-0095.* Always abuzz with Italian families tucking into authentic dishes from tuscany and Umbria.

Fisherman's Grotto $$ *100 Langerman, Kensington; Tel: (011) 622-7272.* Seafood, international cuisine, and pub food, all in a long bar with an enormous wine cellar.

Khazana I $$ *Varsity Place, Jan Smuts Avenue, Bordeaux; Tel: (011) 886-7529.* Mainly north Indian cooking and decor. Clay tandoori ovens are a feature.

Le Canard $$$ *163 Rivonia Road, Morningside, Sandton; Tel: (011) 884-4597.* Award-winning French and international cuisine in a gracious house and garden setting. Also with a notable wine list.

Leipoldt's $$ *Pavilion shopping Centre, corner Rivonia Road and Kelvin Drive, Morningside; Tel: (011) 804-4321.* Cape Dutch and Cape Malay specialities served buffet style.

Ma Cuisine $$$ *40 7th Avenue, Parktown North; Tel: (011) 880-1946.* This splendid French restaurant is a favovurite with local foodies, who flock to taste the perfectly balanced dishes based on the best fresh ingredients..

Mar-e-Sol $$ *Fisherman's Village, Marcia Street, Bruma Lake; Tel: (011) 622-6162.* Portuguese decor and dishes, especially good for seafood with a Mozambique accent.

Daruma $$$ *Sandton Sun Hotel, 5th and Alice streets, Sandton; Tel: (011) 780-5000.* Long regarded as *the* Japanese restaurant in town, Daruma serves a full range of traditional dishes. Reservations essential.

Pescador $$ *Grayston Shopping Centre, Grayston Drive, Sandown; Tel: (011) 884-4429.* Mainly seafood, including Portuguese specialities

PRETORIA

Chagall's at Toulouse $$ *Fountains Valley, Greenkloof; Tel: (012) 341-7511.* International and French bistro-style cooking in elegant country setting.

Chez Patrice $$ *97 Soutpansberg Road, Riviera; Tel: (012) 70-8916.* Creative French and international cooking.

The Odd Plate $$ *262 Rhino Street, Hennops Park, Ext 2, Centurion; Tel: (012) 654-5203.* Training restaurant for South African-born Prue Leith's College of Food and wine, set in a fine old building.

Pachas $$ *Club Centre, 22 Dely Road, Hazelwood; Tel: (012) 46-5063.* International, specializing in fresh fish and shellfish.

DURBAN AREA

Aangan $ *86 Queen Street, City Centre; Tel: (031) 307-1366;* Excellent South Indian vegetarian restaurant with an informal atmosphere.

Ulundi $$$$ *Royal Hotel, 267 Smith Street, Durban, Tel: (031) 304-0331.* Renowned curry restaurant in smart, colonial-style surroundings.

Chatters $$ *32 Hermitage Street, Durban; Tel: (031) 306-1896.* Both creative international and seafood dishes.

Greek Taverna $ *213 Musgrave Road, Berea; Tel: (031) 21-5433.* Authentic Greek dishes and atmosphere.

Le Troquet $$ *Old Main Road, Cowies Hill; Tel: (031) 86-5388.* Bistro-style French cooking.

Leipoldt's $$ *The Workshop, Commercial Road, Durban; Tel: (031) 304-6643.* Wide choice of traditional South African dishes. Closed Sunday evening.

South Africa

O Pescador $$ *Albany Grove, Durban; Tel: (031) 304-4138.* Seafood and other dishes, Portuguese style.

Saagries $$ *Coastlands, West Street, Durban; Tel: (031) 32-7922.* Authentic southern Indian cuisine.

Spaghetti Junction $ *243 Marine Parade, Durban; Tel: (031) 32-4913.* Pasta, pizzas, seafood, and steaks, opposite North Beach.

Taipei $$ *329 West Street, Durban; Tel: (031) 304-6795.* Authentic Cantonese and Taiwanese cuisine. Closed Sunday.

La Dolce Vita $$ *Durban Club, Smith Street, City Centre, Durban; Tel: (031) 301-8161..* Classy Italian cooking in a romantic setting, with verandah tables overlooking the bay.

Villa d'Este $$ *Gillespie Street, Durban; Tel: (031) 37-0264.* Seafood and Italian cuisine, in a courtyard setting close to the beachfront.

PORT ELIZABETH

Bella Napoli $ *Hartman Street, Port Elizabeth; Tel: (041) 585-3819.* Informal Italian and Mediterranean cooking available. Sunday lunch buffet.

Margot's $$ *1 Beach Road, Humewood; Tel: (041) 585-1000.* Creative French, Cajun, and international cuisine.

The Ranch Steakhouse $$ *Russell Road, Port Elizabeth; Tel: (041) 585-9684.* Mainly for steaks, any size, but some Greek and Turkish alternatives too.

Fifth Avenue $$ *Fifth Avenue, Newton Park, Port Elizabeth; Tel: (041) 311618.* Intimate setting and a menu of tasty international classics.

CAPE TOWN AND CAPE PENINSULA

Africa Café $$ *213 Lower Main Road, Observatory; Tel: (021) 447-9553.* Indigenous dishes from across the continent, served in lively, vibrant surroundings.

Biesmiellah $ *Upper Wale Street, Bo-Kaap, Cape Town; Tel. (021) 23-0850;* Traditional Cape Malay dishes, in the old Malay quarter (Hallal Muslim). Closed Sunday.

Constantia Nek $$ *Hout Bay Road, Constantia Nek; Tel: (021) 794-5132.* Between Hout Bay and Constantia. Specializes in functions and dinner-dances. Closed Monday.

Novelli at the Cellars $$$$ *15 Hohenhort Avenue, Constantia; Tel: (021) 794-2137;* Jean-Christophe Novelli's Cape outpost serves delectable, Gallic-influenced food. Award-winning wine list.

The Big Blue $$ *Harbour Road, Hout Bay; Tel: (021) 790-5609.* Informal, mainly seafood restaurant overlooking the harbour.

Dragon Inn $$ *1st Floor, Broadway Building, Foreshore, Cape Town; Tel: (021) 25-3324.* Chinese food, mainly Cantonese, in the city centre. Closed Sunday.

Floris Smit Huijs $$$$ *55 Church Street, City Centre; Tel: (021) 423-3414.* Set in a restored 18th-century townhouse. The menus have an African emphasis with a light modern twist. Closed Sunday.

Fisherman's Cottage $$ *3 Gray Road, Plumstead; Tel: (021) 797-6341.* Mainly, but not only, seafood. Informal setting in southern suburb.

Green Dolphin $$ *Victoria & Albert Arcade, Cape Town; Tel: (021) 21-7471.* Seafood, pastas, and pizzas. Sometimes live jazz. Situated in the redeveloped dockside area.

Miller's Son $$ *10b Kloof Nek Road, Tamboerskloof. Tel: (021) 24-3838.* Mainly seafood. Garden courtyard dining in summer.

Panama Jack's $$ *Royal Yacht Club Basin, off Goliath Road, Dockside; Tel: (021) 447-3992.* Faulous fresh seafood dishes in friendly, informal surroundings.

INDEX

The world's largest collection of visual travel guides

• • • • • • •

Insight Guides provide the complete picture, with expert cultural background, remarkable photography and full coverage of sights and attractions

• • • • • • •

Insight Pocket Guides highlight an author's personal recommendations for the best things to see and do on a short visit. They include a large fold-out map

• • • • • • •

Insight Compact Guides are fact-packed books to carry with you for easy reference when you're on the move. All significant sights are cross-referenced to the maps

• • • • • • •

Berlitz Pocket Guides put the world in your pocket with detailed information, an easy-to-use A–Z of practical advice, eye-catching photography and clear maps

Apa Publications